Occult Bondage and Deliverance

Advice for Counselling the Sick, the Troubled
and the Occultly Oppressed

by
Kurt Koch, Th.D.

KREGEL PUBLICATIONS
Grand Rapids, Michigan 49501

First American Edition 1971

Second Printing 1972

Library of Congress Catalog Card No. 72-160691

ISBN 0-8254-3006-2

Contents

TRANSLATOR'S PREFACE

In spite of knowing the verses in the Bible warning of Satan's attack on the Church, Christians today still find it very difficult to appreciate the battle which is going on around them for their own souls.

The apostle Paul in his letters, warns of people departing from the faith by giving heed to deceitful spirits and doctrines of demons, and, of servants of Satan disguising themselves as servants of righteousness. But of such people he adds: "Even if an angel from heaven should preach a gospel contrary to that which we preached, let him be accursed."

It is in the light of these clear statements of Scripture that this book has been written. Every Christian is a watchman, and therefore every Christian is duty bound to warn the world and his brethren of the dangers surrounding them.

May God, therefore, help those who read these pages to heed the warning, so that they may turn to the One who said: "Behold, I have given you authority to tread upon serpents and scorpions, and over all the power of the enemy; and nothing shall hurt you."

Translator

PART ONE

A. AN EXPLANATION OF THE TERMS

I. *Disease and Demonic Subjection*

Ex. 1. While on a lecture tour of Brazil a few years ago, a young man of 31 came up to me after one of the meetings. He told me that he suffered from severe attacks every fours weeks, in fact during the nights of the full moon. His doctor had tried treating him for epilepsy but there had been no improvement at all in his condition. However, what troubled him most was not so much his strange illness but rather the fact that he found it almost impossible to exercise faith and to pray. After talking with him at considerable length I discovered that both his mother and grandmother had been active charmers. In South America these sorcerers are called the 'bruchos'. The term seems to be derived from the German word 'Brauchen', which means a process of magical charming. Further questioning revealed that my story-teller had been once charmed as a boy against an illness.

As a result of this counselling session the young Brazilian confessed his sins, and in prayer renounced the occult practices of his ancestors. Following this, by the grace of God he was wonderfully healed, or rather delivered.

An example like this, which could be supported by hundreds of similar instances from a ministry which has lasted now for 40 years, raises innumerable problems in the minds of many people.

Many of today's modern theologians and doctors are immediately angered when they hear of epileptic fits and similar attacks being associated with sorcery. A well-known psychiatrist once said, "Theologians should stop meddling in illnesses like this, and leave them to the experts."

Does this mean then that we should just throw in the towel? Never! However, to avoid any misunderstanding arising let me say quite clearly that some forms of epilepsy are entirely explicable in medical terms and are completely unrelated to the sins of sorcery. For instance, the type of epileptic fit that can be localized to a particular part of the brain by means of probes is demonstrably pathological in nature. Let each one of us then keep within the limits of his own practice.

Many Christians already find it difficult to understand why Jesus was prepared to say that certain people were demon possessed, when for all intents and purposes they appeared to be suffering from epilepsy. The so-called experts of today usually retort that Jesus was merely a child of his times. "He didn't know any better, and anyway, the Bible isn't a medical textbook. Today, we are more informed."

However, I find it impossible to accept this present day outlook. Many years of counselling have shown me that Jesus was right in all that he said.

Ex. 2. A minister accompanying me on one of my lecture tours of South America told me the following story. He knew of a family in which one of the children suffered from several attacks of epilepsy each day. When the minister had first met the child he had asked him, "What's your name?" To his immense surprise the child replied in a deep voice, "We are three." After talking with other members of the family the minister came to the conclusion that the child was really possessed, and not suffering from epilepsy. While he was questioning the parents the root cause of the trouble came to the surface, for it transpired that the child had once been cured of a certain illness by means of sorcery, but as a result of this he had developed these fits which the doctor had diagnosed as epilepsy.

In my own experience I have found that this form of 'epilepsy' cannot be treated successfully by medical means since such treatment is simply 'alien' to the complaint. Another example.

Ex. 3. A young married couple came up to me after a meeting and asked to be shown the way to Jesus. The wife had been suffering from epileptic fits for some years. In spite of treatment there had been no improvement in her condition, and so she was finally admitted to a university clinic. They diagnosed that she was suffering from a very rare form of epilepsy called myoklone epilepsy. Since she was the first case the clinic had come across, they treated her free of charge. Various medicines and methods of treatment were tried out on her, and yet, although she returned to the hospital on several occasions to receive new forms of treatment almost as if she were a guinea-pig, there was still no change in her condition. However, counselling revealed that there was one important fact that she had failed to tell the doctors. Her mother had once told her that before her birth she had tried to bring about an abortion by occult means. But the sorcery had not been strong enough. Quite naturally, a doctor, unless he were a genuine and mature Christian, would reject as pure superstition the thought that there can be any connection between epileptic fits and sorcery. Those who only give credence to what their intellects can grasp will be scandalized by an assumption of this nature. And yet the phenomenon exists. We must therefore realize that our human understanding does not supply us with a key to all the secrets of creation.

There are metaphysical and metarational facts, which,

although experienced by man, cannot be explained satisfactorily by him. One is almost forced to the conclusion, as Dr. Lechler has expressed it, that, "If a case of epilepsy can be cured medically, the demonic is not involved. If, however, the illness can be cured by prayer, then it was not an instance of epilepsy."

In the case of the first two examples we quoted the doctors arrived at a false diagnosis. And even in the third case the doctors failed to get to the root of the problem.

The fact that Jesus himself dealt with demonic forms of epilepsy is a confirmation of what we are trying to say. Obviously, though, we are not excluding the possibility of purely pathological forms of epilepsy existing which have no connection whatever with occultism or sorcery.

This brief appraisal of the problems involved should make it quite clear that in order to avoid serious confusion and erronious forms of treatment, one must distinguish very clearly between the facts of medicine and the facts of Christian counselling. Let us not forget therefore:

This book is not dealing with some special branch of psychiatry but rather with one special aspect of Christian counselling as outlined in the Scriptures.

II. *The Question of Competence*

Ex. 4. A few years ago I received an invitation to lecture at a university before a group of doctors and psychiatrists on the problem of possession. In the discussion following the lecture an argument arose concerning a case of possession quoted by a Catholic priest in a book called 'Dämonische Besessenheit heute' (Demonic Possession Today). The symptoms were clearly more in line with the scriptural rather than the medical pattern. Although I am a Protestant myself, I can still recommend this book by Father Rodewyk, a Jesuit priest, for his experiences are very similar to my own in these matters. In the discussion I was mentioning, no one could come to any agreement. When the term 'possession' was used by one of the theologians present, the medical superintendent of a psychiatric clinic sprang to his feet and started exclaiming excitedly, "There's no such thing as possession. The most it can be is some form of hysteria which I maybe haven't come across yet." It was quite clear that this was the general attitude of those of the medical profession who were present. Possession does not exist — and cannot exist! So much for scientific objectiveness!

It is therefore rather useless to expect much help to come from the side of the psychiatrists when dealing with cases of occult oppression, although in England I once experienced a little more understanding.

Ex. 5. The well-known doctor and preacher Dr. Martin Lloyd-Jones had invited me to speak before a group of psychiatrists on the subject of occultism and occult oppression. He invited only Christian psychiatrists to attend the meeting. In the discussion afterwards I was attacked by two psychiatrists who claimed that the biblical accounts of possession I had been quoting were now outdated. They were merely cases of mental illness, as for example hysteria and epilepsy. Again therefore, even in this group one was faced with the usual incredulity and modern form of exegesis. Suddenly, however, another man stood up and came to my defence. He said that his practice was in the area of the New Forest were there was a great deal of sorcery to be found. As a result of this, he said, many of his patients exhibited symptoms that were atypical. On top of this, from his own practice alone he could quote up to eleven different cases of possession. Another psychiatrist then endorsed what his collegue had just said, adding that he had also come across three or four cases of possession himself. I found it unnecessary to defend myself any more.

How is it that while most psychiatrists reject the whole notion of possession, a few not only acknowledge its existence, but can even quote examples of it? The answer to this question is found not so much in the intelligence of the people concerned but rather in their inner attitude. Unfortunately the term 'Christian doctor' is rather misleading. In the light of the Scriptures the word Christian is applicable only to a person who has been born again by the Spirit of God. However, unhappily in Christendom today, born again Christians are often very difficult to find. Yet if a person has not experienced this new birth he is more than likely to say, for example, that the possessed man from Gadara was merely suffering from some form of hysteria, and that the young boy who was 'convulsed terribly' by a demon was only suffering from an epileptic fit. Although interpretations of this nature have a very 'scientific' ring about them, in fact they entirely miss the point.

The Bible refuses to allow us to lower our standards in any way. The Kingdom of God is ruled by a different set of laws to those found in science, and the natural man has no access to them in any way. It is only with the help of the Holy Spirit that we can ever hope to understand the deeper meaning behind the world as we know it. This is not an exaggeration but rather a plain hard fact, for even if all the wisdom of the world were heaped together it would still be foolishness in the sight of God, and God's foolishness would still be wiser than men.

And yet it is extremely encouraging from time to time to meet Christian psychiatrists whose spiritual eyes have been really opened. To this effect a Christian neurologist once said, "60 % of the inmates of my psychiatric clinic are not so much suffering from mental illness as from occult subjection or even demonization." And an English psychiatrist declared once, "If I were able to obtain forgiveness for the sins of the patients in my clinic, I would be able to discharge half of them tomorrow." Statements of this nature imply that many more of our so-called mentally and emotionally ill patients are rather 'ill' towards God than either the public or the medical profession care to recognize. Anyone who is prepared to go into the problem more deeply, will soon realize that many 'mental' and 'emotional' illnesses require the services of an authoritative Christian counsellor rather than a rationalistic medical doctor.

The question of competence will never come to an end. Both sides are guilty of erronious conclusions and false diagnoses. However, since we know that Jesus himself never erred in his judgement, we know too that those who enter the school of Christ and are filled with the Holy Spirit will be able to lay hold of a portion of his garment, and that through this others will be healed in much the same way as the woman who experienced a miracle in her body when she reached out to touch the Lord.

Yet medical science must be given its rightful place, for it too, is of God. But at the same time we must not allow our right to spiritual and charismatic counselling to be taken away from us. Both have their rightful place. And it is often extremely beneficial for the two to work side by side in cases where the diagnosis is doubtful. In this way everyone should use that gift which he has received from God.

An experience I had in France illustrates quite clearly and typically the question of competence.

Ex. 6. A psychiatrist came to see me while I was holding a series of meetings in France. He was a believing Christian and wanted to tell me of a really wonderful

event that had occurred in connection with his work.
A woman had suddenly gone out of her mind in a nearby
village and had had to be forcibly restrained by some
of her relatives. The vicar had been called in and he
happened to be a young modern theologian whom I knew
quite well. In fact he had attacked my views quite strongly
once at a mission I had been holding. This young minister
had advised the family to call in a psychiatrist at once,
and he had given them the name of my story-teller. The
psychiatrist, on his arrival, had given the patient a strong
sedative in the form of an injection. Since this appeared
to have no effect on the woman, he gave her a second
injection 20 minutes later. But again there was no change
in her condition. Thus over a period of two hours the
psychiatrist in fact gave the woman four doses of the
same sedative without there being any apparent diminish-
ing of her muscular activity. On this the doctor turned
to the minister and said to him, "Vicar, I have given
her the strongest dose possible. This isn't a case of
mental illness, she must be possessed. If she had been
mentally ill, she would have shown some reaction to the
injections I have given her by now. Medicine therefore
won't be of any avail. The only thing that can help her
is prayer."

I am glad, although not in any vindictive sort of way,
that this young modernist was taught a lesson by the
psychiatrist. It is refreshing to hear of a theologian having
to be told by a qualified doctor that a patient's troubles
have a spiritual cause for which a purely medical form
of treatment is inadequate.

This French psychiatrist is, however, not the only
person in his profession to believe in the reality of demon
possession. Dr. Lechler himself, and the Swiss author and
physician Dr. Paul Tournier, both belong to this
distinguished group of doctors. In the United States the
psychiatrist Dr. William S. Reed makes no secret of his

convictions concerning the demonic, and is recorded as having said, "Many mental and physical illnesses result, in fact, from demonic attacks. Exorcism must therefore be given a place within present day psychiatry and medicine." This is a brave statement to make but it has already brought Dr. Reed into a lot of conflict with those who can only accept what to them is 'rational'.

Finally in this connection let me mention just one other person who belongs to quite another camp. A great stir was caused in Sweden by the book of a certain spiritistic doctor by the name of Dr. Wickland. Before anyone jumps to any false conclusions let me say straight away that I am absolutely opposed to spiritism, no matter what form it takes. However, occasionally one finds a grain of truth even in the enemy's camp. In his book Dr. Wickland tried to show that the majority of mental illnesses are a type of demonic possession.

If anyone reflects for a moment on what these Christian psychiatrists have had to say, or even as a last resort on what this spiritistic doctor has written about, one will perhaps be able to sense why psychiatry in particular must be considered to be still in a state of infancy. While both medicine and surgery seem to be enjoying almost unheard of successes today, psychiatry is, so to speak, still at the stage of learning its ABC. One of the reasons for this is the fact that the subject of the demonic is either completely overlooked or merely explained away in terms of superstition. But I dare say, that by making a remark like that I will quickly be accused of wanting to return to the Middle Ages.

III. Occultism

First of all we will begin by considering the actual meaning of the word 'occult'. It is derived from the Latin word occultus and means: hidden, secret, dark, mysterious, concealed. It is used to describe those phenomena which either transcend or seem to transcend the world of the five senses.

Occultism as a part of folklore has been practised for thousands of years. There are two main features characteristic of all the material I have been able to collect on this subject from the 120 or so different countries I have visited during the 40 years of my ministry. Historically speaking, the rules of occultism have remained unchanged throughout all the different epochs of man. The actual practices of occultism are the same today as they were 5000 years ago. Second to this is the fact that no matter what the level of civilization, the methods used by that civilization remain the same. The form may change, but the underlying principles remain unchanged.

If space permitted I could illustrate this with hundreds of examples drawn from all over the world. Suffice it to say that the shaman Alualuk, whom I met in Alaska, used the same methods and the same powers in his occult practices as his colleagues in the tropical heat of the Amazon jungles. They differed but in name, for in the area of the Amazon they are called the kahontschi. In Jamaica they are called the obiahs, in Bali, Indonesia, the dukun or bahan. On Hawaii the black magicians call themselves the kahuna, and on the Fiji Islands the drunikau. In spite of their racial, linguistic, geographical and cultural differences all of these are skilled in the same arts. The very real similarity between their practices has puzzled ethnologists, anthropologists and psychologists a great deal.

For this reason it has been suggested that these magical and occult forces are an example of a primitive ability of man which has gradually become stunted over the course of the centuries.

It was Prof. C. G. Jung of Zurich who introduced the

idea of archetypes. He suggested that hidden behind the causality of the world of the psyche there lies an a-causal reality in which space and time lose their meaning, and where the laws of cause and effect cease to apply.

But we can only barely touch on the subject here. However, it is obvious that in the West and in the universities of our world today the dominating outlook is a rationalistic one, whereas in Asia, Africa and to a large extent South America, the people are governed rather by a mediumistic picture of the world. For the purposes of this book our approach to this subject must be of a purely practical nature, immediately helpful in the area of Christian counselling.

Let me illustrate, however, the difference between the rationalistic and the mediumistic by means of just one example from the mission field. And let me say again that every example I have quoted in this book is either drawn from my own personal experience or has been passed on to me by another Christian worker from his own field of activity.

Ex. 7. When I was in Thailand once, a missionary told me the following story. One of the elders in his church injured his hand and subsequently developed blood-poisoning. The infection spread extremely quickly in the tropical climate. A dark-red, almost black streak started moving up his arm. However, since the nearest field doctor lived a considerable distance away, the native Christian hesitated somewhat before going to see him. When he did finally visit the doctor, the dark streak had already reached his shoulder. The startled man was told immediately, "You must go to the hospital. That arm will have to be amputated, otherwise you'll be dead by the morning." The church elder was taken by jeep to the hospital and the surgeon confirmed what the doctor had said. The arm had to come off if he wanted his life to be saved. The poor rice farmer replied, "But I need my arm.

How will I be able to look after my rice fields without it?" A terrible battle started raging within his heart. It was then that he remembered an old Hindu sorcerer who it was claimed was able to heal people by means of mysterious powers. Although the elder knew from the missionary that it was forbidden for Christians to consult with sorcerers, his despair drove him on. It turned out that the Hindu was by no means a fake, for his magical powers really worked. The blood-poisoning was halted, and the arm was saved. But the resulting effect in the native Christian's life was that he ceased attending the meetings of the church and gradually slipped back into heathenism.

An example like this clearly contrasts the difference between rationalistic and mediumistic remedies. Where reason comes to an end, the occult can sometimes still supply an answer. Yet the overall effects are well-known. The church elder had to forfeit his relationship with God.

For years I have witnessed the truth of this fact, that magic and almost all other occult practices either destroy the Christian faith of a person or just prevent it from developing. And yet one finds that there is no conflict between sorcery and all the other world religions. This does not mean that magic is more powerful than the Christian faith. No, it merely shows that those who occupy themselves with occult practices are in fact contravening the laws of God.

IV. *Occult Activities*

From the thousands of examples I have collected, three main divisions become apparent. These are: fortune-telling — magic — spiritism. One can split each of these main divisions into a further 20 to 40 subdivisions. Since, however, I have already gone into this subject in some detail in other of my books, only a brief summary is necessary here.

1. *Fortune-telling* includes:

a) The use of a rod and pendulum (radiasthesia). Archaeologists maintain that this practice is more than 7000 years old. They base their conclusions on the date assigned to the cave drawings to be found in the Orange Free State, although personally I would query this date, for archaeologists today are for ever being forced to reassess and post-date their findings.

b) Astrology. One can include under the heading of astrology the popular idea of horoscopes, astromantic, and cosmobiology. These can be dated with certainty at least back to the third millenium before Christ, and astrology can be traced through the Sumerians, the Chaldeans, the Babylonians, the Greeks and the Romans right on up to the present day.

c) Palmistry. This art was invented by the Babylonian priests and goes back for a period of 4000 years.

d) Card-laying. The Romans were the first to use this as a form of fortune-telling, the cards they used being in the form of small wax tablets. Paper playing cards as we know them, first came into use around the year 800 AD.

e) Psychometric clairvoyance. This too began at the time of the Romans and has continued to the present day. It would take too long, however, to go into all the other forms of fortune-telling one could mention.

We must never forget, though, that in the area of the occult there are many frauds, swindlers and charlatans. It is probable that more than 90 % of all fortune-telling is really faked. Let us not therefore be deluded into thinking that all forms of fortune-telling are genuine just because a few brilliant predictions come true.

Ex. 8. I can illustrate the problem quite briefly by means

of a single example. A young man had his hand read by a gypsy. She predicted three things. "Your father," she said, "is going to win a large sum of money. But he is going to die when he is 60." As the young man laughed in disbelief, the woman went on, "And you will only reach the age of 27!" A few years later the young man heard that his father had won about £ 5,000. Then on his father's sixtieth birthday he received a telegram saying that his father had had a fatal accident that very day. The fear of the third prophecy being fulfilled now began to take hold of the young man.

There are a number of problems that face us in an experience like this. First of all, should we not consider it a part of God's mercy that he has hidden the future from us? Would not man live in continual fear if he knew what the future held? But from where did the gypsy obtain her prophetic foresight? She could not have read of the father's death in the palm of his son. Here it was a case of genuine contact with the world of darkness. It is not in vain that the Scriptures say, "Anyone who practises divination, a soothsayer, or an augur . . . . is an abomination to the Lord." The price the young man had to pay for his deed was exceedingly high.

2. *Magic* includes:

The healing and the inflicting of diseases; love and hate magic; curses; fertility charms; persecution and defence magic; banning and loosing; death magic.

The actual word magic is not uniformly defined and therefore we will explain here exactly what we mean by the term.

Some people talk of the magic of music, or the magic of art and of sport, and even the magic of love and religious cults. But we are not dealing here with this meaning of the word magic in its widest sense.

Then we have so-called magical tricks, performances in

magic, magic circles and so on. But this form of magic does not concern us either.

The only form of magic we are dealing with in this book is the age old art of sorcery and magic mentioned in the Bible, the actual cult of demons performed in collaboration with the powers of darkness.

Two examples can be used in order to actually introduce us to the problem.

Ex. 9. A young girl working on a farm had an illigitimate child by the son of her employer. She told him that he should marry her, but the son refused. Because of this the girl cursed him with the words, "When you marry and have children, your first child will be born an idiot and your second child will die an unnatural death." Both the curses came true.

For the sake of the reader let it immediately be said that if we place ourselves under the protection of the blood of Christ no such curse as this can ever harm us. On the contrary, I know of examples where a curse put on a child of God has actually recoiled and struck back at the person who invoked it.

It should also be pointed out that behind both curses and blessings there is to be found a great deal more than mere words. Both the Bible and counselling reveal this clearly. If anyone is interested in reading more on this subject, I would recommend him to read the small booklet by Dr. Lechler called 'Fluchen und Lästern' (Swearing and Cursing).

The worst area of magic that exists is that of death magic. Scientists naturally look upon this as sheer superstition and humbug, but I have in front of me enough examples from all over the world to prove exactly the opposite. When a practising magician is converted and becomes a Christian he often makes a clean breast of his past life during the course of his confession. It is at such times that one discovers the real truth concerning magic and sorcery. I am actually acquainted with two forms of death magic, both of which are paralleled by similar Christian phenomena in the New Testament. On one occasion the apostle Peter, prompted by the Holy Spirit, foretold the deaths of Ananias and Saphira, and his words came true. On other occasions we read of both Jesus and his disciples raising the dead to life again by the power of God.

The devil is ever seeking to imitate God, thus one finds that in the same way as God can sentence to death and raise to life again, so too the devil by means of sorcery can do the same thing. Having already written at length on the subject in my other books, it will be sufficient here just to quote a second example.

Ex. 10. The most powerful sorcerer I have ever met is the shaman Alualuk whom, as I have already mentioned, I met in Alaska when visiting the Eskimo tribe to which he belongs. This shaman even possessed the occult power to raise heathen people from the dead. One such person who he raised to life again lived a further ten years. However, Alualuk was soundly converted to Christ and as a result of his conversion he lost his magical powers. When I asked him, "Whose power did you use to do all these things?" he replied, "The power of the devil of course." He admitted, though, that he had never possessed any power over real and genuine Christians.

Throughout the testimonies of former magicians the same comforting message continually recurs. Jesus Christ has defeated all the powers of darkness. The true believer is therefore for ever guarded by Him from all the devices of the devil. However, a merely nominal Christian who carelessly comes into contact with the occult is in serious danger of falling prey to a satanic ban.

3. *Spiritism* (necromancy, spirit communication).

It would be impossible to consider in detail all the subsidiary forms of this demonic cult. The most well-known forms include: table lifting; glass moving, speaking in trance; automatic writing; excursion of the soul; materialization; telekinesis; apports; levitation; spiritistic cults; spiritualism and so on. Anyone desiring to have more information concerning these various forms of spiritism should turn to the two books 'Between Christ and Satan' and 'The Devil's Alphabet'. We will not be repeating here what has already been written in these two previous publications. To give an indication, however, of at least part of the area involved we will quote just two examples.

Ex. 11. During one of my visits to the United States I came across a book by Edgar Cayce called 'The Sleeping Prophet'. This particular paperback became a best seller and has run through numerous editions and sold over a million copies. Edgar Cayce's fame resulted from both his success as a healer and the fulfillment of his prophecies. Unfortunately many Christians are still being deceived by his success since they are unable to distinguish clearly between the gifts of the Spirit and purely mediumistic powers.

People in America who wanted either help or healing, merely wrote a letter to the 'prophet'. Cayce would then concentrate on the letter and fall into a trance. In the trance he would be able to discover the exact complaint of the person requiring help, and at the same time would be able to bring the person within his healing influence. In a similar way he was also able to find articles which had been lost and make accurate predictions concerning the future.

Since his powers were only liberated when he was in a trance, he was given the title 'the sleeping prophet'. Yet there are two basic errors to be found in the title itself.

First of all he was not asleep but in a trance — there is a clear distinction between the two, because when a person is asleep for example, he can be woken up by the prick of a needle, whereas a person in a trance will feel nothing. The second error is in the word prophet, for Cayce was not a prophet in the true sense of the word, but rather a sorcerer. In the Acts of the Apostles we find that Simon Magus and Elymas were also magicians or sorcerers, and could in no way have been called men of God. But today we live in such a chaotic age that terms are confused and interchanged and the devil is often given the honour instead of God. The argument that is often put forward, that Cayce was able to alleviate the suffering of many people, is a very superficial one. In fact, he was the means of oppressing many. Cayce was only a spiritist and a mediumistic trance healer. He has thereby rendered the American nation a bad service. It cannot be denied that many of his healings were a great success, but the Bible itself talks of demonic signs and wonders being performed (Matt. 24 : 24; 2 Thess. 2 : 9). Thus any relief obtained is only partial and the subsequent oppression is very costly.

Ex. 12. The second example is a source of much joy to me. The story is that of one of my friends who came to my aid once while I was engaged in a difficult argument at a meeting in London. At the close of this meeting an Anglican minister had attacked me and attempted to defend the religious form of spiritism called spiritualism. It was then that Mr. Millen had risen to his feet. "For many years," he said, "I was a spiritualistic medium. When I was in a trance I was able to diagnose and to heal diseases, and at seances I could be transfigured into the forms of other people. Yet the power enabling me to do all this was that of the devil, and I was in his grip. However, my wife used to meet together with a group of Christians in order to pray for me. They continued to do this regularly until the Lord Jesus performed a miracle in my life. I was delivered from the powers of darkness and became a Christian myself."

His testimony was extremely encouraging to hear. Mr. Millen had come to my defence in a very bitter attack. But the triumph of the gospel is the fact that even those who are heavily bound by the devil's power can be gloriously liberated by the power of Christ. If this were not so, the courage would fail me to write about this difficult form of counselling work.

Spiritism can be found in many different forms and guises. Animistic spiritism speaks of awakening the unconscious powers of a person's mind. The spiritistic form talks of 'spirit guides' and 'operators' from the other side. Criminal forms of spiritism, as for example the Macumba cult in Brazil, lack all restraint and practise the basest forms of evil imaginable. Social types of spiritism as typified by the Kardec spiritists are responsible for the building of schools, hospitals, and similar institutions. And the religious form of spiritism, better known as spiritualism, claims to be in possession of the highest and ultimate revelation of God. And yet every one of these forms is based upon a common demonic foundation, including those who hide their wares behind a show of good works. In Deut. 18 : 11 God says quite explicitly, "There shall not be found among you anyone who practises divination, or a medium, or a necromancer. For whoever does these things is an abomination to the Lord."

This then brings us to an end of our brief description of the main divisions of occultism. We have not had time to mention the extensive area covered by other superstitious beliefs and practices which run into thousands. To oppose the world of true Christian faith and belief, the devil has evolved the world of superstition and occultism. The Civitas Dei, the Kingdom of God, is confronted by the civitas diaboli, the kingdom of Satan.

But this is not a form of dualism. Satan is not a rival of God nor an equal to God. He can only act within the limits which God has set for him, and only with such powers as the Lord permits. Yet as an enemy he is dangerous. Without the protection and the saving power of the Lord Jesus Christ, no human being would be able to withstand the attacks of the prince of darkness.

V. *Parapsychology*

Scientific research has recently shown a great deal of interest in so-called supernatural phenomena. The very name of this new science, parapsychology, is indicative of its nearness (para) to psychology itself.

This awakening of scientific interest in the occult world led to the founding of the 'Society for Psychical Research' in 1882 in England. Later, scientific institutes sprang up all over the world in order to do research into parapsychological phenomena:

1934 at Duke University in the United States (Prof. Rhine), and at Utrecht in Holland (Prof. Tenhaeff),

1954 at Freiburg in Germany (Prof. Bender),

1960 at Leningrad in Russia (Prof. Wassiliew), and finally

1964 at Santiago in Chile (Prof. Onetto).

I have already been asked quite frequently concerning my opinion of parapsychological science. But one reason I am reluctant to state it, is that I have on a number of occasions been attacked quite bitterly by parapsychologists on the radio, on the television, and at public meetings. Let me, though, ask my questioners to consider the following. In their scientific research, parapsychologists are forced to investigate all sorts of occult phenomena. Thus, for example, they participate in spiritistic seances and make experiments with mediums, a practice against which God Himself has warned in the Bible. These scientists, however, completely disregard this warning in their determination to investigate the powers of spiritistic mediums. But are they exempt from the laws of God? Are they of all people immune to the dangers and injuries which God has ordained will befall those who sit in spiritistic circles?

But the problem is even more complicated. While lecturing in both England and the United States, I discovered that some well-known clergymen are not only members of these parapsychological societies and institutions, but sometimes even chairmen. An example.

Ex. 13. A senior English clergyman is a member of the Society for Psychical Research. An Anglican minister once went to see this clergyman to ask him for his advice in dealing with a haunted house. The minister was recommended to take a spiritistic medium with him to the house in order to discover the reason for the haunting. This he did, and it transpired that the previous owner of the house, through having been ill-treated there, was still frequenting the place in order to frighten the future inhabitants. But the story does not end there. On another occasion the Anglican minister informed the clergyman that he felt as if he were being personally attacked by the powers of darkness. He was thereupon given some white magic formulae and charms with which to defend himself. I was told all this by the Anglican minister himself.

Now what does all this mean?

1. A well-known clergyman is not only interested in parapsychological research, but is also a member of the aforementioned society.
2. A theologian who should be well acquainted with his Bible, tells a colleague to go and seek the help of a medium.
3. This so-called man of the Bible recommends the use of white magic as a means of defence against the attacks of the devil.

This example alone is sufficient to give one an idea of the width of the problem.

In my own counselling work I have already quite frequently been forced to witness the actual results of certain parapsychological experimentations. Up till now I have always resisted the temptation to publicize this and similar information, but let me now just give one example.

Ex. 14. Over the last few years certain parapsychologists have made a number of experiments with the famous Dutch clairvoyant Croiset. Croiset's abilities have often enabled him to help the police with information which has led to the solving of a number of crimes, the discovering of corpses, and the clearing up of not a few mysteries. But I have had to personally counsel many people who have actually been to Croiset to receive his clairvoyant services. These people have told me that they will never go to him again, for following their visit to him they became troubled and confused in their minds, and in particular, their spiritual lives suffered a great deal. I could quote examples of this in detail, yet parapsychologists are unwilling to admit the truth of these things, for if they did so they would be unable to pursue their experiments into clairvoyance and spiritistic mediumship with a clear conscience.

Although this section on parapsychology is bound to provoke a good deal of ill feeling, I have been forced to write in the way I do, since a warning on this subject is long overdue.

Perhaps at this point we can single out one particular problem which should shed some light on the whole background of parapsychology. Parapsychology divides all occult phenomena up into two specific groups: the psi gamma phenomena and the psi kappa phenomena. The word psi is an abbreviation for the word parapsychological, while gamma stands for the Greek word gignoskein = to know or to recognize, and kappa represents the Greek word kinein = to move. This introduces us at once to the problem of the knowledge and the motivating force behind the extrasensory. It was these very two areas which were mentioned by the serpent in the garden of Eden. In Genesis 3 : 5 it is written, "You will be like God, knowing . . ." This is Satan's proposition: knowledge and power through obedience to the serpent. And basically all the phenomena of occultism are to do with the question of obtaining new knowledge and new power, be it fortune-telling, magic or spiritism. Yet these extrasensory faculties — obtained in both unnatural and ungodly ways — are today the subject of scientific research. And so, with a complete lack of foresight, experiments are conducted in all these areas. What good, we ask, can result from this? What fruit can be derived from merely playing with fire?

One is naturally driven to ask these questions, however, not because one considers the problem from a purely 'scientific' point of view, but rather because our ideas must be shaped according to the faith we find recorded in the Bible.

VI. *Occult Subjection*

First of all let it be said that there are many forms of oppression which are undoubtedly readily recognizable by the medical profession. For example, it is known that the children of a notorious drunkard are usually 'visited' with the same sin as their father. And a manic-depressive usually passes his melancholic disposition onto his descendants. Similarly mentally ill people suffering from incurable psychoses should be recommended not to marry, for we tend to inherit not only the good but also the bad hereditary factors of our forefathers. A book I can recommend people to read on this subject is one by Prof. Pfahler, called 'Der Mensch und seine Vergangenheit' (Man and his Past).

However, if one talks to scientists today on the matter of occult subjection, it is often almost like talking to a brick wall. Any psychiatrist who is not a truly born again Christian would simply deny the existence of occult subjection and oppression. At most they may possibly retort, "One must be very careful not to confuse the cause with the effect, and vica versa. Superstitious people are capable of almost anything. The oppression is the root cause, the occult involvement is only secondary."

Yet in my fourty years of Christian work, and as a result of having counselled something in the region of 20,000 individual people, I have personally come across thousands of cases in which it was the contact with occultism that was the root cause of the problem, and the oppression that was the direct result of this contact. In the light of this, I have often wondered why the scientific research workers of today have been unable to produce any form of argument or proof in support of their dogmatic a priori assumptions.

Let me illustrate what I mean. For years now the well-known thalidomide court process has been going on. The actual firm that made the drug manufactured something in the region of 30 million individual doses. However, the press has only reported something like 3,000 cases of thalidomide children being born. This is a ratio of one in ten thousand, which means that for every 10,000 doses of the drug sold, only one thalidomide child has been born. And so the case against the firm has yet to be proved.

Now, if we were to consider the number of cases in which occultism has had a damaging effect on people, our ratio would work out to something in the region of nine out of ten cases. I could support this fact by means of many thousands of examples. Yet scientists persist in saying, "The problem does not exist." If one's counselling work were dependent upon narrow-mindedness like this, one would be driven to despair. Yet we should not be surprised. Although Jesus was able to heal lepers, non-Christians among the medical profession and modern theologians still cry, "It's impossible." Similarly, although Jesus was able to raise the dead and came back to life again Himself, the same cry goes up, "Impossible." If then this is the attitude people have towards Jesus, we should not, as his insignificant disciples, be worried if we too have to face the same shortsighted criticism.

We must not forget: occult subjection is not a medical term but rather a concept and idea connected with the Christian faith. For this reason it is the Christian counsellor alone who is qualified to deal with this particular problem, and not the qualified medical doctor. However, as we saw in Ex. 6, occasionally, instead of the minister being the counsellor, the task can fall to the Christian doctor.

As has been pointed out already, a number of Christian psychiatrists do in fact acknowledge the existence of the demonic and are familiar with the problem of occult subjection. It may be of interest if I quote two more examples of this at this stage.

Ex. 15. While lecturing just recently in New Zealand, I heard some very good reports of a certain psychiatrist living in Hamilton. He is the son of a minister and the brother of a bishop. This doctor claims that 50 % of the neurotics being treated in the clinics in Hamilton are the fruit of Maori sorcery. The Maoris are the original inhabitants of New Zealand and there are many sorcerers to be found in their ranks.

Ex. 16. I made the acquaintance of another psychiatrist while visiting the town of Suva on the Fiji Islands. He told me that the drunikau, the name given to the sorcerers in that area, saw to it that the psychiatric clinic there was never lacking in patients. He then gave me a few examples. If a drunikau tells one of the natives, "You'll die before sunset," the victim always dies. Neither

the relatives nor the psychiatrist is able to talk the unhappy man out of his delusion.

Ex. 17. On the island of Bali the percentage of inmates
attributed to sorcery is even greater. I have been able to
hold meetings in five different places on the island and
came across some terrible examples of occult oppression.
In Denpasar one doctor told me, "85 % of our patients are
neurotic." This is not surprising since a great deal of
black magic is practised on Bali. It is not in vain that
the missionaries call the island, the island of the devil.

Often while I have been touring the Far East and the
Pacific Islands, educated men have complained to me of
the arrogant attitude of Western scientists, and how
they simply explain away all mediumistic phenomena as
harmless, without really knowing the slightest thing
about the background or the effects of these phenomena.

There are obviously notable exceptions to this rule.
Dr. Lechler himself is an example of this. In fact, during
his 35 years as the medical superintendent of the largest
mental hospital in Germany, through both his medical
work and his work as a Christian counsellor, he learnt
to divide occult subjection into four stages of oppression.

1. The simple form of occult subjection which can
   remain unnoticed for years until subsequent events
   uncover it.
2. Demonization in which a reaction immediately occurs to any form of Christian counselling.
3. Obsession, whereby the person is continually surrounded and controlled by the powers of darkness.
4. Possession, the state a person finds himself in when
   actually indwelt by demons and evil spirits.

These four stages of oppression form a unity. They
are merely different intensities of the same phenomenon.
And let it be pointed out once more that Dr. Lechler himself actually believes in the possibility of a person being
literally possessed by demons.

VII. *The Effects of Occult Subjection*

First of all, what is the basic cause of occult sub-jection? Every sin connected with sorcery cuts a person off from God and turns him towards the worship of idols. And if a person begins to serve the devil, he will receive the devil's wages. Thus, when a person abandons God, he abandons himself at the same time. There are innumerable passages in the Bible declaring quite clearly that sorcery and occultism are terrible sins which are an abomination to the Lord and a forsaking of the living God. The following are but a few of these passages:

Exod. 7:11—12	1 Sam. 28
Exod. 22:19	2 Chron. 10:13—14
Lev. 19:26, 31	Isaiah 2:6; 8:19
Lev. 20:6, 27	Jer. 27:9, 10
Zech. 10:2	Gal. 5:20
Mal. 3:5	2 Tim. 3:8
Acts 8:9	Rev. 21:8
Acts 16:16	Rev. 22:15
Acts 19:19	

Anyone who trespasses into Satans domain by com-mitting sins of sorcery will immediately be harassed by the powers of darkness, irrespective of whether he takes the step consciously or unconsciously. And the effects of this transgression of God's laws make themselves felt in five different areas of a person's life.

1. The oppression is most clearly seen in a person's *spiritual life* and in his faith. But the question which immediately arises is, what faith? Is the Moslem's faith, the Buddhist's faith and the Hindu's faith affected as well? No, this is the strange thing about sorcery. It is only Christians, and to a lesser extent God-fearing Jews, who are affected. All the other religious faiths of the world seem to ally themselves to mediumistic phenomena.

Only the Christian faith stands out in sharp contrast to occultism.

It follows then that any person who has resorted to fortune-telling, or magic, or spiritism in his life, will find it very difficult to turn to Christ at a later date. He will be unable to obtain any assurance of salvation or peace with God. And if perchance he has already become a Christian, he will find that a coldness and a kind of ban will descend upon his Christian life. He will lose his desire to pray and to read the Bible, and will become lukewarm and sluggish in his faith. Or, on the other hand, he may become hypocritical and selfrighteous and Pharisaical as a result of his contact with occultism.

Ex. 18. A man who had been charmed on several occasions in his youth later married a Christian girl. Although he himself went to church at times, he had no real personal relationship with God. His young wife soon realized that her husband had no real desire to pray together with her, and had little interest in living the Christian life. On account of this she formed a prayer group which continued to pray for her husband for a number of years. In the end, at a certain mission, he was suddenly awoken to his need and he came to see me after one of the meetings. A terrible battle immediately commenced during which time he thought he was almost going mad. He had no peace either day or night, so much so that he even tried to commit suicide. Yet in spite of taking enough poison to kill three people, his life was saved, and in a subsequent counselling session he asked me, "Why can't I become a Christian, because I really want to?" As I questioned him further, it came to light that he had been charmed as a young boy.

This example illustrates the fact that quite frequently occultly subjected people are able to live peacefully so long as they remain in the 'world'. Only when the desire to be born again enters their heart does the trouble start.

The rule is quite simple: the devil will not trouble a person so long as he remains his servant. Only when his victim wants to leave his 'school' does the resistance begin. Then when the conflict actually commences, since many occultly subjected people almost go out of their minds, the natural result is that unbelieving relatives, and in the end the doctor himself, start saying, "Well, that's what you get through praying too much. Stay away from church for a while and stop reading your Bible until you get better." How often are the times when I have heard of this advice being given, but the only thing it proves is that the one giving it knows nothing of the laws of the spiritual life outlined in the Bible.

Every form of sorcery is in reality a contract with the powers of darkness. The devil therefore accepts this as his right to take people captive, and will resist strongly at the first hint of his having to lose his victim.

2. Occult subjection also effects the *character* of the person concerned. As a result of sorcery one can be plagued by fits of temper and fury, quarrelsomeness, avarice, and a domineering personality. Such people are unsociable and can exhibit all forms of exaggerated passions, including alcoholic addiction and licentiousness. Many compulsive criminals are to be found within this group of people, which is exemplified by the fact that in the Lüneburger Heath in Germany a man once set ten houses on fire without knowing what he was doing. It turned out that his grandfather had been able to charm people as well as animals. Obviously, however, the judge never asked him about this, for no one ever guessed there could be any connection.

3. Another marked characteristic of occult oppression is the fact that many people suddenly become melancholic immediately after their conversion. An example of this.

Ex. 19. A 21-year-old woman told me while I was counselling her that she had become a Christian two

years previously. Since her conversion, however, she had
started to be plagued by depressions, a lack of desire to
live, and even thoughts of suicide. In fact she had twice
tried to take her own life. Yet all the troubles had only
started after her actual conversion. As I talked with her,
it came to the surface that both her mother and grandmother were still actively engaged in laying cards for
people.

Occultly subjected people frequently begin to show
signs of all sorts of *emotional disturbances* when they
begin to think about surrendering their lives to Christ.
However, we must be very careful to point out at this
juncture that emotional illnesses, depressions, neuroses
and suicidal thoughts can have many other causes apart
from that of occult involvement.

For example certain depressions, known as endogenous
depressions, depend on the disposition and the hereditary
factors of the person concerned.

Next we have a group of depressions known as reactive
depressions which are related to recognizable stresses in
the patient's life. For example an excessively strict
upbringing can later produce depressions in a sensitive
child, and a young girl expecting an illegitimate child
can as a result of her fear and shame become depressive
and try to commit suicide.

Then, and this is particularly important to remember,
there is a group of depressive illnesses entirely dependent
upon pathological and organic causes. Certain heart
diseases can result in depressions, and a liver complaint
can sometimes produce mental and emotional disturbances
as a kind of side-effect. In the same way excessive dieting
can also trigger off a series of depressions, and a change
in the activity of the endocrine glands may well effect
the emotional life of the patient.

One must therefore be very careful of not falling into
the trap of believing that every depression is a sign

of occult subjection. Occult subjection is in fact only one cause among maybe twenty different causes of mental and emotional disorder. Ignorance of this fact, together with all too hasty conclusions, often lead to disastrous results when counselling people.

It is always advisable for a person to have had some form of medical training if he is going to engage in this type of counselling work. However, in spite of this there are certain basic points which make it possible for someone unqualified in medicine to distinguish fairly clearly between the depressions we have just been mentioning. Depressions resulting from occult involvement usually make their appearance immediately after a person is converted, or when they first come into contact with some form of Christian influence. This phenomenon is known under the name of resistance. However, a lifetime of experience is really required before one can with certainty differentiate between all the various shades of depression that exist, and even then there is always more to learn. Although blasphemous thoughts and a feeling of abhorrence to the things of God can arise in conjunction with depressions resulting from occultism, blasphemous thoughts in themselves are no proof that the occult is involved since they occur quite frequently in other forms of mental illness. For example, in the case of people with an exceptionally sensitive conscience, blasphemous thoughts can arise in their minds as a form of inversion. But we have not got time to go into details concerning this psychological problem.

Summarizing the four groups of depressions we have just mentioned, we have:

endogenous (through disposition and inheritance),
reactive (as a result of stress in the person's life),
organically based (resulting from illness) and
occultly caused (through sorcery etc.) depressions.

4. Many years of experience have shown me that families in which sorcery has been practised are much more prone to *mental illness* and mental abnormalities than other families. An example of this.

Ex. 20. A woman came to me in Canada and told me some most absurd things. She claimed that the neighbours had dug tunnels under her house in order to spy on her. When I asked her to show me the tunnels, she replied, "I can't, because they are under the cellar and in the walls." She went on, "They've ground my stone floor down during the night by more than 8 inches." "But why haven't you called the police in?" I asked, to which she replied, "But when they do it they give me an anaesthetic, and it's just as if I'm paralysed." It is not necessary here to make a list of all her phantasies. Every psychiatrist is familiar with hundreds of stories similar to this. It was a case of an unshakable delusion which one often experiences with paranoid illnesses and certain forms of schizophrenia. It was notable that the woman was otherwise a very highly intelligent person. She was a teacher. As I questioned her it appeared that her father for years had practised glass moving as a form of party game.

What I am trying to say is in no way meant to be a criticism of these families, but is only meant to point out the simple observation that spiritistic families are more susceptible to mental illness than other families. Now, please do not misunderstand what I am saying. Spiritism itself is not to be regarded as the direct cause of the mental illness, but is rather productive of a form of oppression which in turn triggers off certain mental and emotional disturbances. The spiritistic and demonic cults of spiritism in fact act as a kind of catalyst in the mental structure of the human personality.

5. Another phenomenon symptomatic of occult involvement is the development of *mediumistic abilities*.

However, this expression, mediumistic, is quite difficult to define. It is derived from the Latin word medium = middle, intermediary, mean. A medium is a person who mediates between unseen forces — and in the case of spiritism between invisible spirits, and the world of man. There is a great need in the Western world for a book to be written on the subject of mediumism from the Christian point of view. What in the East is understood as easily as the ABC, meets with complete incredulity and disbelief in the West. One could say that perhaps 90 to 95 % of the people in the East are already mediumistically inclined, while in the West the percentage is perhaps in the region of 5 % or less. This mediumism is often possessed unconsciously by people, but certain events and certain experiments allow one to recognize its presence. Yet I would warn people very strongly against taking part in any such experiments, for one can easily become infected through them.

Mediumism itself can develope in three different ways. That is, either through inheritance, or through experimenting with magic and spiritism, or finally, through transference. Let me explain briefly. If a person's grandfather, for example, was a spiritist or a magician, then not only his children but sometimes both his grandchildren and great-grandchildren can be born with mediumistic tendencies. Later, if one of his descendants is converted, his mediumistic abilities may suddenly disappear, although in about half the cases they usually remain. That means that a Christian can have mediumistic abilities without really knowing it. Nevertheless, a real Christian can quickly be liberated from this mediumship whenever he wishes.

One of the worst things that can happen, however, is for a disciple of Christ to suddenly discover one day that he has these abilities, and then for him to assume that they are some form of charismatic power given to him

by the Holy Spirit. Two famous examples of this are
to be found in William Branham and Oral Roberts. People
make a terrible mistake when they come to regard these
mediumistic abilities as instruments of the Holy Spirit.
But to write all I could on this particular subject would
go beyond the bounds of this book.

Secondly, mediumism can be acquired through magical
experimentation. Anyone allowing himself to be healed
by means of occult powers usually becomes mediumistic
afterwards. In the same way if a person consults or uses
books on sorcery over a number of years, he will certainly
develope mediumistic abilities.

Then thirdly, mediumism can develop as a result of
transference. If a person with a strong radiasthetic ability
grips the hands of a person with no such ability and
teaches him to use a rod or a pendulum, the latter will
usually end up with the same mediumistic ability as the
former. However, such transferences are easy to prevent.
For the first thing one should in no wise consult or have
any contact with a mediumistic practitioner, and secondly
mediumistic powers can always be nullified through
prayer.

Mediumism itself takes on about ten different forms.
These include: radiasthesia (the ability to use a rod or
pendulum), second sight, dream fulfillment, clairvoyance,
clairsentience, trancelike states, mesmeric healing powers,
and suggestion and hypnosis both of which can be
mediumistically based. Although certain Christian workers
believe that some types of healing mesmerism are
dependent on neutral rather than mediumistic powers,
I would say that I have personally hardly ever come
across a neutral form. Many years of experience in this
field have shown me that even in the case of Christian
mesmerisers the basic mediumship has always come to
the surface in the end. And telepathy, too, belongs to
the world of mediumistic abilities. To prove this I have

innumerable examples, but in the case of telepathy I have discovered that neutral forms also actually exist.

Ex. 21. One excellent example of this comes from a friend of mine who is the chief of a tribe of aborigines in Australia. His father and grandfather are both still alive, and they too are leaders in the tribe. Being leaders these men have telepathic power to give orders to the whole tribe, even when the tribe is spread over an area ranging into hundreds of square miles. The same method of communication exists in Lapland also. But what I learnt for the first time in Australia was that the chiefs, by the use of particular call signs, are able to contact any individual member of the tribe they want to. The member being called knows immediately who is 'on the other end of the line'. Now the young chief had become a Christian. In fact he was the first member of his tribe to be converted. When I stayed with him for a period of some weeks, I found him to be a very sincere and honest young man. I asked him once, "Did you lose your telepathic powers when you became a Christian?" "Not completely," he replied. "I have lost the ability to call up individual members of the tribe, but I can still communicate with members of my own family. And my parents and brothers and sisters can still contact me." I then asked him, "What do you think gives you the ability to do this?" "The power to contact the whole tribe," he said, "was demonic. That's why I lost it when I was converted. But the contact I still have with my own family must be natural, because they can even get in contact with me when I am on my knees praying."

It is remarkable that in Scandinavia the Lapps possess exactly the same ability as the aborigines in Australia, an ability which I have already described in the book 'The Devil's Alphabet'. From the racial point of view they are completely unrelated. The Lapps are basically a white race, whereas the aborigines are either black or dark skinned. The mediumism, in this case the telepathy, must therefore be a phenomenon very basic to the human race. This the Christian will be readily able to understand, for he will recognize at once the actual power lying behind it.

Over the years it has become quite obvious to me through my counselling work that all these mediumistic abilities are really a diabolical counterpart to the spiritual gifts bestowed on us by God. The devil is ever trying to imitate God. One can justify this conclusion by the fact that mediumistic forces and powers can always be overcome and halted through the prayers of a believing Christian. Similarly the actual possession of mediumistic abilities is always a hinderance to the development of a sound and healthy Christian life. Therefore, as we have mentioned already, there is nothing worse than when mediumistic powers are ignorantly accepted and labelled as evidences of the workings of the Holy Spirit. And yet this is exactly what is happening among certain extreme Christian groups today.

VIII. *Mediumistic Healing*

Mediumistic forces are equally as dangerous, even when they are being used for a supposedly humanitarian or social reason, as is the case with the so-called spiritual healers of today. These healers are to be found in almost every country one visits, and their powers, almost without exception, are of a mediumistic nature. Now some examples.

Ex. 22. I came across the story of an 'astral surgeon' in the Philippines. Spiritists believe, that as well as having a material body, man also possesses an astral body. This particular man, it was claimed, was able to do operations on the astral bodies of people. Without the use of any instruments he merely manipulated with his hands above the person's body. The whole idea seems at first sight ridiculous, but let us have a look at the results of such operations.

One woman who was known through X-rays to be suffering from gall stones, went and visited this astral surgeon. Subsequently new X-rays showed that the stones had disappeared. It was a case of some sort of spiritistic apport, an apport being the appearance or disappearance of an object within a closed space. It may perhaps also have been an example of dematerialization, where substance just disintegrates and dissolves into nothing.

Were it not for the terrible oppression which follows, such an operation would be the desire of all those who suffer from kidney stones and gall stones. But the organic healing is compensated for by the most severe psychical complications. I once counselled a man who had undergone such an astral operation. He told me that for months following the operation he had had to visit a psychotherapist without, however, receiving the slightest help.

Ex. 23. In Germany there is a spiritual healer by the name of Dr. Trampler. I have heard many reports of this man's work through having counselled former patients of his. It appears that during the consultation he stands in front of the patients, concentrates for a few seconds, and then accurately diagnoses their complaints. After this he brings his mediumistic powers to bear upon them, and then asks, "Can you feel a warmth coming over you?"

The process of healing commences with the initial clairvoyant diagnosis and is then followed by a psychical-mediumistic influencing. The resultant effects become apparent when the people subsequently seek the advice of a Christian counsellor. I was told by one Christian woman that because she had prayed in his consulting room, Dr. Trampler had sent her away with the words, "I can't help you at all."

Ex. 24. During my various visits to England I have frequently come across the tracks of one of the most dangerous healers of the Western world. His name is Harry Edwards. Thousands of people have been brought under his spell and burdened as a result of his spiritistic practice. We must therefore acquaint ourselves a little with his work. The facts I shall be quoting are all taken from a biography of Harry Edwards published by the Spiritualist Press. The source is therefore authentic.

Edwards, who today calls himself a spiritual healer, first visited a spiritualistic meeting when he was in his early forties. In 1934 he attended his second seance accompanied by his wife and a friend. These meetings are a very common phenomenon in England. He was soon told at the seances that there were spirit guides who wished to co-operate with him. But at first he detected no changes in himself, although at later sittings he felt an inner force welling up inside attempting to take control of him. In this way it seemed to him as if spirits used his subconscious reactions "to promote mediumship under some form of spirit possession through the domination of his subconscious mind."

As time went on he became more and more subject to the control of his so-called spirit guides, and as his mediumship grew he gave a number of trance addresses at various spiritualistic churches.

The book makes no mention of any experience of conversion or turning to Christ in the life of Edwards.

It was about this time that he had his first experience of absent healing. He was told by a friend about a person who was suffering from consumption, pleurisy and haemorrhage. As he started his initial attempt at absent treatment, he had a vision of a hospital ward and he was able to see the patient clearly. Later he was informed that on the very night he had commenced healing, the victim of consumption had begun to improve: his fever had abated, his haemorrhage stopped and the pleurisy ceased.

It is quite englightening to find the book itself pointing out that Edwards' healing power stems from his spirit guides on the other side. Equally enlightening is the book's assertion that spiritual healing has nothing to do with "the Christian theory of vicarious atonement, under which Jesus was supposed to take all the sins of mankind on his shoulders." We should be very grateful to the author for this clarification. It should at least make it clear to everyone that the healing movement associated with Harry Edwards is completely unrelated to both Christ and the Bible.

Concerning his method of healing, the book has the following to say: "He sought a trance condition during which the healing guide would be present, and not until then would the healing begin. He would make the sweeping passes. . . . and follow with movements applied to the seat of the trouble." Although over the years his mode of healing has gradually become less spectacular, the actual source of his healing powers has always remained the same.

Besides his healing ministry, this famous healer has also taken part in hundreds of seances and spiritualistic meetings, during which he has personally witnessed materializations, apports and many similar spiritistic phenomena.

As a result of his continual contact and work with fellow mediums, Edwards' mediumistic powers increased from year to year. Gradually as his fame spread, doctors and even clergymen began to turn to him for help. The book claims that the number of ministers has run into hundreds. Edwards is also the president of the National

Federation of Spiritual Healers, a body which now has over 2,000 members. His postbag sometimes reaches the phenomenal figure of 12,000 letters a week and 10,000 are considered a fair average. In addition to his 'absent healing' he has also developed the ability to travel out of his physical body to the place where his patient is, the so-called art of spirit travelling or excursion of the soul. Today he conducts most of his absent healing during the night, beginning his work maybe at midnight when most of those who have sought healing are asleep and their minds still. Yet how he manages to answer 10,000 requests for healing each week is a little hard to imagine. Perhaps his method is similar to that of Gröning who used to choose a special time in which to think about all his patients generally. To crown his success, members of the Spiritualistic Federation were granted permission, subject to the consent of the doctor in charge, to give treatment in over 1,700 British hospitals to patients who requested their services.

And then, at the end of the book, the biographer concludes his remarks with the following sentence: "In my view this is the same divine power which streamed through the healer of Nazareth in Bible days and produced results that the orthodox regard as miracles."

Seen from the scriptural point of view this is a terrible confusion of spirits. It is in effect the equation of spiritistic forces and demonic revelations with the work of the Holy Spirit. In spite of the Bible designating spiritism as the cult of the devil, and in spite of it condemning those who take part in spiritistic practices, here is a man who, after having taken part in hundreds of spiritistic meetings, still claims to be a channel of divine power. It seems unimaginable that genuine Christians should ever resort to such a person for help, and yet while counselling people in England I came across the case of a British missionary actually sending her own mother to

Harry Edwards in order to obtain healing. What terrible shortsightedness and irresponsibility.

But quite obviously healings do take place. The question is, what is the force behind the healing? We have many passages in the Bible recording the ability of sorcerers to work miracles. We need only think of the Egyptian magicians who opposed Moses in Exodus 7, or of the demonic signs and wonders mentioned in Matthew 24:24, Mark 13:22, 2 Thessalonians 2:9 and Revelation 13:13 and 16:14.

Every person healed through the influence of mediumistic forces, though, suffers a deathlike blow to his faith. He falls victim to a kind of spiritistic ban. And this will be particularly tragic in the case of the many hundreds of ministers and clergymen who have turned to Harry Edwards for this extremely doubtful type of help.

Edwards has rendered the British people a dreadful service. Thousands upon thousands of people have been burdened through the work of this prophet of spiritistic spirits. And yet the Christians in England remain silent.

Ex. 25. I will quote just one example to illustrate more clearly the dangers involved in turning to this particular healer for help. I was once asked to speak at the church of a certain Anglican minister in England. During the discussion after the meeting I was attacked quite strongly by some spiritualists in the audience. They attempted to prove that Jesus had been the greatest medium who had ever lived, but I told them this was blasphemy. Another member of the audience then stood up and started objecting to what I had been speaking about with the words, "But there's nothing wrong with white magic and spiritualism. In fact, they do a lot of good. And besides, Moses and Elijah only appeared on the mount of transfiguration by means of spiritualistic methods. You can only understand the New Testament correctly if you regard it from the spiritualistic point of view." I found it difficult to

get a word in edgeways in my own defence, but then
suddenly a Christian married couple sprang to my aid.
They told the audience of their own experience with
Harry Edwards. "When we bought the house we last
lived in," they began, "we discovered that Harry Edwards
had been the previous owner, although at the time we
were unaware who he really was. Hardly had we moved
into the house, however, than we started to experience
strange ghostlike phenomena and to hear odd noises about
the house. The house made us feel continually ill at ease
and we felt very oppressed. In the end we decided to
move. Then one day a man from Durban in South Africa
suddenly turned up at our doorstep. Immediately he
entered the house, he started saying, "This is wonderful.
You have spirits here. I want to buy the house." However, in spite of the fact that he was prepared to pay
anything for the house, we felt it would be wrong to
sell it to him, and subsequently sold the house through
an estate agent. It had just become impossible to live
with the spirits any longer. Later we discovered that Harry
Edwards had become well-known as a spiritual healer,
and although we learnt that innumerable people visited
him daily in order to receive help, and that some were
prepared to pay anything up to £10,000 to be treated
by him, we knew from our own experience the true
background of his so-called healing powers."

But at this stage we must turn our attention to another
healer we have mentioned, William Branham, a man who
possessed exceptional mediumistic abilities. Yet someone
will no doubt ask, why can't we leave the dead in peace?
The truth is that spiritually speaking, Branham is not
dead. His sermons are still being published today in
Germany. I have even been sent them myself through
the post, although I never requested them.

In one way, although Branham also used mediumistic
powers, he cannot be compared with the English spiritual

healer Harry Edwards, for unlike Edwards he was at the same time a Bible preacher. I have actually heard him preach myself, and although his messages were a little extreme, they were not altogether completely uninteresting. But, for example, concerning the fall of man in the garden of Eden, he claimed that Cain was the son of a union between Eve and the serpent, and that only Abel was the true son of Adam. This is quite a repulsive theory for which the Bible offers no proof. If anyone doubts what I am saying, they can actually find this written in one of the printed sermons I have just described.

Branham's healing powers, however, had much in common with the healing ability of Edwards. The following story was told to me by one of the first people who interpreted for Branham. By this I do not mean the Rev. Hollenweger, but rather an American-German minister R. This born again Christian minister told me the following.

Ex. 26. Branham said to him one evening just before a meeting, "Don't stand to the right of me because my angel stands there." The interpreter asked him quite innocently, "What does your angel look like?" Branham went on to describe a well-built man with dark hair who stood with folded arms next to him. He had to obey whatever the angel said to him.

On occasions Branham would arrive late at a meeting. When the interpreter encouraged him to try and arrive earlier, Branham replied, "I can only do what my angel tells me to do. He's with me day and night and if I don't do what he says, I have no authority in my preaching. I can't even decide things in my own private life, and can only go out or see people if the angel allows me to."

The interpreter went on to tell me that Branham would sometimes fall into a trance when he spoke and that later when he had finished preaching, he would be completely exhausted. His son would have to massage his back until he felt better again.

At the end of his meetings when people came to the front to seek healing, the angel had always told him who to lay hands on and who to send away. In fact Branham was merely a slave of his angel.

Once the interpreter asked him, "Do you think your power to heal people comes from the Holy Spirit?" "No," Branham replied, "my angel does it."

When he discovered this, my story-teller stopped working for Branham. "If I had known previously what had been going on," he told me, "I would never have accepted the job in the first place."

Although some of the more simple of Branham's followers might accept that his angel was a genuine angel of God, I find this impossible to believe myself. On the contrary, all the evidence points in the opposite direction. Angelic appearances in the Bible have an entirely different character to this. The angel's presence and the authority Branham received through the angel are very similar to the phenomena experienced by the healers of the spiritualistic churches in England and America. Harry Edwards himself was only able to heal people when his spirit guides had presented themselves with him.

If anyone believes I am doing William Branham an injustice, he should turn to an account of his conversion which will be similarly interspersed with such unbiblical accounts of angelic visions. And besides, I have several hundreds of pages of material which are quite sufficient to enable one to assess the matter fairly. Perhaps I can quote one further example just to open people's eyes a little more.

Ex. 27. I have quite often had the opportunity to speak in churches in Los Angeles. After one particular meeting, a doctor's wife came up to me and told me the following story.

Her brother-in-law, in spite of being a minister, had got involved a great deal in occultism. He took an active part in spiritistic meetings, in magic and similar occupations. He was also fairly friendly with certain extreme Pentecostal groups, and as a result of this he came into contact with Branham. When they were first introduced, Branham exclaimed quite spontaneously, "You look exactly like the angel which appears to me every day." The Christians who knew this weird spiritistic minister were afraid of him. His six brothers had forbidden him to enter their homes, and his sister-in-law, the doctor's wife who was telling me the story, had also refused him entry on one occasion. The next day, however, eczema had broken out in eight different places on her body, and she blamed this on Branham's spiritistic friend, since she knew quite well that he was able to both heal and inflict diseases upon people.

This example again gives us confirmation of the fact that Branham's angel was a spiritistic rather than a divine angel. Although a number of Branham's followers maintain that by saying this, one is in effect blaspheming, one could produce a great deal more evidence supporting this view. The Rev. Otto Witt made a grave mistake when he openly praised Branham's life and work.

We are living today in a time of much chaos. The final stages of world history are rushing upon us as the coming of Christ draws near. The powers of darkness are spreading, so much so that even born again Christians are finding it difficult to see their way clearly. Let us therefore not forget the warning of the apostle Paul in 2 Corinthians 11:14 where he writes, "Satan disguises himself as an angel of light. So it is not strange if his servants also disguise themselves as servants of righteousness."

Mediumistic abilities have nothing to do with the gifts and the fruit of the Holy Spirit, even when they make their appearance in the guise of religion.

Throughout the world one finds that spiritualists and spiritists usually argue in the following way: "There are not only evil spirits in the world but also good spirits. We consort with the good and ward off the evil." Yet this statement is a contradiction in itself. Good spirits know and recognize the laws of God and will refuse to trespass beyond the limits set them. They know that God has forbidden spiritism and has labelled it a demonic cult, and hence they would never allow themselves to be drawn into either the practices of spiritism or spiritualism. As angels of God, they obey their Lord. Indeed the Bible says, "Are they not all ministering spirits sent forth to serve for the sake of those who are to obtain salvation?" (Heb. 1:14). The genuine appearance of an angel is accompanied by characteristics entirely different from the spiritistical spirit and angel accounts of Harry Edwards and William Branham.

In Germany there is one book in particular I can recommend on the subject of angels and demons. It is written by Hermann Leitz and published by Missionsverlag in Bad Liebenzell.

I come now to a painful duty I have put off for many years. However, after a great deal of prayer, I feel I must fulfil the obligation which God has placed on me.

In the autumn of 1966 together with about 2,000 other delegates, observers and staff members, I attended the World Congress on Evangelism in Berlin. Among the leaders of the various discussion groups was Oral Roberts, a man who had been publically greeted by Billy Graham on the platform. As a fellow delegate I wrote to the committee informing them of the fact that the healing ability of Oral Roberts was of a mediumistic rather than a charismatic nature.

The letter caused a lot of anger among those who read it and the next day Billy Graham introduced Oral Roberts a second time to the great audience, putting his arm round his shoulder and addressing him by the name of brother. I have been troubled for some years now by this lack of discernment on the part of Billy Graham and his committee. Previously I have been unprepared to write about it for fear of damaging their work, a work which I personally value, and which I in no wise wish to hinder. However, on account of the immense amount of damage which is being caused by Oral Roberts in many areas of the world, I feel unable to remain silent any longer. When Dr. Edman, the late chancellor of Wheaton College and friend of Billy Graham was still alive, I talked with him about this problem. He was readily able to understand and appreciate the warning I wanted to give. I also spoke to John Bolten, the treasurer of the Billy Graham team, at Schloß Mittersill in Germany. My desire was that these men, as two of the closest friends of Billy Graham, would speak to him personally about the matter, but as yet I do not know what the outcome has been. Billy Graham is in fact a man whom God has been able to use mightily throughout the world. As an evangelist he commands a greater audience for the Gospel than almost any other person alive. It would be incorrect to question the work of a man in his position whom God is blessing so much. Yet even great men can make mistakes. Not every person has all the gifts of the Holy Spirit. My prayer is therefore that in the light of the harmful activities of Oral Roberts, Billy Graham will be given a greater gift of discernment in these matters. To argue that Oral Roberts has founded a university, or has collected millions of dollars for the kingdom of heaven, is no proof that he derived his healing ability from God. It could just as easily be said that, since Harry Edwards has collected thousands of pounds for his healing ministry and has become the leader of an organisation numbering over 2,000 spiritual healers, his powers must be of divine origin, which is patently not true. And so, only after a great deal of prayer and after a number of unsuccessful attempts to warn both Billy Graham and his friends, am I forced to bring these things to the notice of the Christian public at large. And I speak as one who has been able to witness the negative effects of the work of Oral Roberts in a number of countries throughout the world.

Although Oral Roberts is probably unaware of the fact himself, his power to heal is more indicative of a mediumistic ability than a gift of the Holy Spirit. It is possible that he originally received these mediumistic powers from the old Indian who once healed him in his younger days. He actually spoke about this at the Berlin Congress.

Although a number of people have begged me urgently to publish examples of his healing ability, I am still unwilling to go into detailed accounts of his ministry, for I do not want a book on counselling to be filled with negative examples. It is the Lord Jesus and not man to whom we should listen, and to whom we should give the right to speak. Nevertheless as a warning to Christians I will quote just three examples concerned with his work.

Ex. 28. One of the most terrible stories relating to Oral Roberts came to me through a believing minister who is himself much used of the Lord. Together with his father-in-law who is also a Christian, he went to one of Oral Roberts' meetings. What he wrote to me afterwards is too terrible to recount in full, so I will quote only the last few lines of his letter. "I am certain about one thing though, there is a great deal of swindle buried beneath the arrogant performances of Oral Roberts. Thank God that if our Christian faith is sound, by following the inner guidance of the Lord and by adopting the correct biblical attitude, we will be able to experience case upon case of healing by faith. In this situation there is no question of following a blueprint as 'divine healers' so often do."

Ex. 29. Once when I was holding a series of meetings

in Singapore, a Christian missionary told me about one of Oral Roberts' healing campaigns. Roberts had told a young man, "In the name of Jesus you are healed." Later, however, it appeared that he had not been cured. His father therefore, a quick-tempered Malay, took a revolver and went to find the 'lying healer' as he called him, in order to shoot him. Fortunately by this time Oral Roberts had already left the country.

Ex. 30. During the Berlin Congress on Evangelism another very significant event took place. It was during a meeting of one of the subcommittees and Oral Roberts was the leader. There were about 300 delegates present including the Rev. Pagel, the evangelist Leo Janz and myself. Roberts had been speaking on the subject of healing when one of the Americans present asked him, "Mr. Roberts, isn't it true that during your television programs you have sometimes asked the viewers to place a glass of water on the television during the actual broadcast?" After receiving an affirmative answer, his questioner went on, "And isn't it also true that at the end of the programs you have told the viewers to drink the water if they are seeking healing?" Again, in the presence of the 300 or so delegates Oral Roberts replied, "Yes." That was honest of him. But what type of healing is this? Occasionally during similar programs one of the viewers has been asked to place his hand on the television set and with his free hand to either touch or to form a chain with the other viewers present. But this is the sort of practice one finds in connection with spiritistic table-lifting, when chains are formed in order to encourage the flow of mediumistic forces.

Where is the actual atmosphere of the New Testament here? This is rather just the kind of hectic climate in which the suggestive or religious-suggestive ideas are being bred that masquerade today under the name of faith-healing.

Ex. 31. Another evangelist found within the ranks of today's faith-healers once spoke to a group of aborigines in the northwest of Australia. One of the bushmen present was a born again Christian. After listening to the messages of the evangelist for a few evenings, he suddenly cried out, "Lord Jesus, where are you? I can't find you here. There's nothing for me at these meetings." With that he got up and walked out of the service. Here is the case of a primitive and uneducated man possessing a gift, the gift of discernment, which one often looks for in vain among the so-called great people in the Christian world.

Ex. 32. In the past, men of God seemed to have a great deal more discernment concerning the danger of mediumistic forces than the great evangelists of today. Henry Drummond, the friend and fellow worker of D. L. Moody, was one such man. Before his conversion Drummond had possessed some very strong mediumistic and suggestive powers. He thought that these ungodly endowments would disappear when he became a Christian, and yet to his astonishment, he found that his mediumistic abilities reappeared while he was working together with Moody. He discovered for example that he was able to hypnotically influence a person who was maybe 50 miles away, and he also noticed that he was able to bring the large audiences at Moody's meetings under his hypnotic influence. He recognized at once that these powers would only hinder the actual working of the Holy Spirit, and he therefore pleaded with the Lord to take them away from him. Drummond was completely delivered. One wonders, however, what the result would have been if he had not recognized the potential danger of his mediumistic talents. His whole ministry together with that of Moody's could have been damaged. This example clearly indicates that a Christian can still be dogged by his mediumistic powers even after conversion. For this reason, those who are in active service for their Lord have a great need of the gift of discernment, for unless they have this gift, their whole work is in danger of suffering from strange additives which can only cause a great deal of harm in the Kingdom of God. The sin of the sons of Aaron, Nadab and Abihu, is occurring today over and over again as people offer their 'strange fire' in the service of the Lord (Lev. 10:1, 2).

O God, preserve us from walking contrary to your ways, and send your fire to consume all that hinders the work of your Holy Spirit.

IX. *Possession*

Since the medical question is going to be dealt with in the second part of this book, we need not repeat ourselves here. As we have said, however, for the non-Christian psychiatrist possession just does not exist. At most it is only an advanced form of hysteria. But attitudes like this need not worry us. Possession is a religious and spiritual phenomenon which needs to be regarded and judged from a spiritual point of view.

1. The symptoms of possession.

For anyone desiring to consider the phenomenon of possession, a study of the story of the Gadarene demoniac in Mark 5 is essential. Eight distinct symptoms of possession are described there.

Mark 5:2	The demoniac had an unclean spirit. In other words, he was indwelt by another being.
Mark 5:3	The possessed man exhibited unusual powers of physical strength. No one could bind him any more.

Mark 5:4   The third characteristic was the paroxysms
            (the fits of rage). He had wrenched chains
            apart and broken his fetters in pieces.

Mark 5:6, 7 The fourth sign is one of distintegration,
            the splitting of the personality. The de-
            moniac runs to Jesus for help, yet cries out
            in fear.

Mark 5:7   The fifth sign is that of resistance, an
            opposition to the Christian faith and
            spiritual things. He tells Jesus to leave him
            alone. One meets this resistance to spir-
            itual help quite often in counselling sub-
            jected people.

Mark 5:7   The sixth symptom is hyperaesthesia, an
            excessive sensibility. The Gadarene had
            clairvoyant powers. He knew immediately
            who Jesus really was.

Mark 5:9   The seventh sign is seen in the variation
            or alteration of voice. A 'legion' of demons
            spoke out of him.

Mark 5:13   The eighth characteristic is occult trans-
            ference. The demons left the man and
            entered into the swine.

It should be noted that the second, third and fourth
characteristics we have just outlined, are similar in many
respects to the symptoms of certain mental illnesses.
However, I say similar, for in no case are they exactly
the same. The remaining five characteristics on the other
hand are not to be found within any psychiatric
classification. For example clairvoyance itself is never
a sign of mental illness, and a mental patient will never
be able to speak in a voice or a language he has previously
not learned. Yet this is exactly what has happened and
still does happen in some cases of possession, when the
possessed person during one of his attacks suddenly

begins to speak in a language or languages of which he has had no previous knowledge.

In a similar way, transference never occurs in connection with the mentally ill, but only with the obsessed or possessed. Some examples can be used to illustrate what I mean.

Ex. 33. The late Friedrich Heitmüller, a man who was much blessed of God, told me the following story. He was once invited to visit the house of another Christian. The Christian's son had been showing signs of possession. Heitmüller had taken along two other brothers, one of them a Christian teacher and the other his son. Together they had prayed with the possessed boy and then in the name of Jesus had commanded the powers to leave. The result was that the boy had been delivered, but from that moment the teacher's son present with them, had become possessed. What had happened? They had thought that the young man had been a believer, but later it was discovered that he had never become a real Christian. A transfer of evil powers had therefore taken place.

This kind of transference never occurs in the realm of psychiatry. Nevertheless there are certain circumstances when something vaguely similar to this takes place, although the nature of this second type of transference is entirely different.

I have frequently met people who, as a result of caring for the mentally ill in psychiatric clinics have themselves become the victims of emotional and mental disturbances. In fact I know of two well-known professors of psychiatric medicine who as a result of such mental stress finally committed suicide. One of them was Professor S. of Heidelberg and the other a professor in Amsterdam. What is the difference between these two forms of transference?

In the case of possession, the one who was originally possessed is always delivered, while a non-Christian or nominal Christian present at the time of exorcism becomes indwelt and possessed by the evil spirit of the former.

In the case of transferences involving mental illness, the original patient experiences no change in his condition, while the doctor or nurse attending him begins to suffer from mental disturbances at the same time.

Ex. 34. One Easter Monday about ten years ago a young man came to visit me. Although I explained quite clearly how he could become a Christian, something seemed to prevent him taking the final step. When we prayed together though, he suddenly fell to the floor and another voice began to speak from him saying, "Dr. Koch, you have four children. Give one of them to me and I will leave this man alone." The voice spoke of the young man in the third person. I replied, "My children are all protected by Christ. You can't have any of them. Go to the place where Jesus sends you." The voice now asked, "There's a drunkard in the pub nearby. Let me go into him and then I'll leave this chap." Again I answered, "You can't go into the drunkard either. Go to the place where Jesus sends you." Yet again for a third time the voice asked me, "Then let me go into some pigs." But my reply was the same, "Go where Jesus sends you." In counselling possessed people I have never had the freedom to send a demon to the abyss. This is something outside my jurisdiction.

Ex. 35. In Switzerland a well-known evangelist once came to me and told me that his own father had become deeply involved in sorcery. As a result of this he had become demonized, if not actually possessed. However, when another Christian worker had visited their house, his father had been converted and had accepted the Lord Jesus as his Saviour. But when this had happened, their five pigs had suddenly started running around madly in their stall. They had kept this up for hours, squealing all the time. In the end, not being able to pacify them, they had had to shoot all five. I realize that an example like this will cause ripples of laughter to pass through the ranks of our rationalist friends. But we must let them. The wisdom of this world is foolishness with God, and as Paul the apostle said, "God will destroy the wisdom of the wise, and the cleverness of the clever he will thwart" (1. Cor. 1:19).

It is a strange thing, but one often finds more understanding in the Catholic Church towards the problem of possession than in Protestant churches. This statement is all the more important for I myself am not a Catholic. In the Catholic liturgical book called 'Rituale Romanum Tit. X' four signa (symptoms) of possession are listed. These are:

a) Knowledge of a language not previously known,
b) Knowledge of secret and remote things,
c) Manifestation of unnatural powers of strength,
d) Aversion towards the things of God and the Church.

2. How can possession be recognized?

I have been asked on numerous occasions at either ministers' conferences or during church meetings about the way one can recognize cases of demonic possession. What, people ask, is the actual difference between mental illness and demonization or possession? This is one of the most difficult questions facing people engaged in counselling work.

My first piece of advice to anyone who asks this question is, "Before all else make sure you have surrendered your own life to Christ. Next ask God for the enlightenment of the Holy Spirit. Then if possible undergo some form of medical training." It is our duty to make use of everything that God has given us to help us in our task. This includes our reason, our experience, and most of all a heart born again and filled with the Holy Spirit.

But the question arises, is it possible for people with no medical training to recognize a case of possession when they see it? Yes, for there are certain signs one may look for which we have already mentioned. However, we can expand upon this a little.

There is first of all a very simple rule one can adopt. If one meets a person who claims to be demon possessed, then he is not demon possessed. Anyone who is really possessed will neither realize nor broadcast the fact of his possession.

Next one must remember that as a result of ill-informed or extremist forms of counselling some people are almost talked into believing that they are possessed. One must be aware of the fact that within some of the more extremist groups of Christians, and this particularly applies to some of the more exaggerated Pentecostal groups, this suggested form of possession is almost forcibly inbred into people. Christians must be clearly warned of this fact, and on no account should an occultly subjected person be taken along to one of these groups when deliverance is sought. The only effect would be to make the person's condition worse.

But please, do not misunderstand me when I say this. I have met many sincere and sacrificial children of God within the more moderate and sober Pentecostal churches. In many countries in fact it is these churches that contain the most active Christian workers. Unfortunately, however, the number of extreme or so-called 'wild' Pentecostals outweighs the number of truly scripturally orientated Christians in the movement. And these extreme religious groups are a breeding ground for all sorts of neuroses and depressions. One wonders how many people, instead of being helped, are instead burdened and oppressed further after receiving the laying on of hands from mediumistically endowed Pentecostal evangelists. Now for some examples.

Ex. 36. A Christian woman came to me to ask for my advice. After having been a Christian for many years,

a Pentecostal evangelist had one day visited the town
in which she lived. She went along to his meetings. One
evening the evangelist had said that if anyone wanted
to receive the baptism of the Holy Spirit they should stay
behind after the meeting. The woman had stayed behind
and had received the laying on of hands. However,
although she was afterwards able to speak in tongues,
she lost her peace of mind and her assurance of salvation.
As a result of this, she had come to me for counselling,
since she felt that something had gone wrong in her
life. She repented of her action and renounced her new
experience. Following this she lost the ability to speak in
tongues, but regained her peace of mind and her
assurance.

Ex. 37. In San Diego, California, another woman came
to me for counselling. She too had gone along to a
Pentecostal mission where she had been told that unless
she had spoken in tongues, she had not been filled with
the Holy Spirit. However, on receiving the laying on of
hands, she had fallen into a state of unconsciousness.
Afterwards she discovered that all the peace she had
ever had, had gone. Her everyday life became filled with
strange attacks and temptations, so much so that she
came to the conclusion that the laying on of hands she
had received, could not have been of God. After talking
with her for a while she asked God for forgiveness and
regained her assurance of salvation. She never visited
that particular Pentecostal group again.

Ex. 38. A Christian girl on account of an illness went
along to a Pentecostally run convalescent home. During
a period of counselling she was prayed for under the
laying on of hands. But she was not healed. The next day
the minister laid hands on her again, but there was still
no change in her condition. Because of this the man said
to her, "You have a devil. You are possessed." The girl
left the home in despair, believing herself to be possessed.

She had been the victim of a dreadful and unforgivable piece of counselling. Never in my life have I ever said to a person, "You are demon possessed," even on the occasions when I have actually felt this to be the case. We have no right whatsoever to confront a person with so grave a diagnosis as this. At most one can form a prayer group for the person, telling those who take part that the symptoms point to a possible case of possession. Yet personally till now I have never even adopted this procedure. We can pray for a person without having to say what we think is wrong with him. One cannot approach the world of evil spirits and demons in such an off-hand way. It cost Jesus his life when he made an end to the powers of darkness on the cross. And who are we compared to him? We must be very careful not to start jumping to conclusions in this area, and thereby become the victims of a kind of occult neurosis. We need not blame occultism and demons immediately something goes wrong in our own lives, and we should guard against labelling others as occultly oppressed when we have no proof of the fact that they are. All too often people label events as demonic for which there is a quite natural explanation.

Having made this very necessary appeal, we can now turn our attention back to the characteristic signs of genuine cases of demon possession. In my counselling of possessed people throughout the world, one is always confronted by the same main criteria. These are four in number.

a) The phenomenon of resistance. What do we mean by this? If one prays with a person who is merely suffering from a mental illness, he will quieten down when one prays. On the other hand, if one prays in the presence of a possessed person, he will begin to build up a resistance and become angry and violent, and start to curse and blaspheme and threaten to hit out at the counsellor if he does not stop praying. He may even start to spit, or tear a Bible up and throw it across the room. Yet when the counsellor finishes his prayer, the person will often apologize and exclaim, "I didn't want to do that. Something just made me do it."

In these circumstances a mentally ill person and a possessed person exhibit entirely different behaviour patterns.

Ex. 39. A young man came to me for counselling. I showed him the way to Christ and we began to pray together. Suddenly he jumped up and started running and banging his head against the wall time and time again, as if he wanted to kill himself. After I stopped praying, he asked me to forgive him his behaviour with the words, "I didn't want to do that. It just came over me." On talking to him further, I discovered that he had worked at the office of an astrologer. Calling in two other believing Christian men, we together commanded the evil powers to leave the young man. He was delivered.

b) A possessed person can easily fall into a state of trance during a time of prayer. The devil refuses to allow his victims to listen to either the Word of God or to prayer, and he therefore simply cuts him off from the source of spiritual help through making him fall into unconsciousness. Mentally ill people never react in this manner.

Ex. 40. In Zurich a minister brought a woman along to me to be counselled. As we prayed together the woman started sticking her tongue out at us and blaspheming. We noticed that when she was doing this, she was not completely conscious and as we finished praying she suddenly came to herself and asked, "Where am I? What's wrong with me?" She could remember nothing of what had just taken place.

Ex. 41. In the Philippines I was counselling a young

Bible student. When I prayed with him and mentioned the name of Jesus, he just fell to the floor. Suddenly a different voice cried out of him in English, "Don't mention that name. Don't mention it. I can't stand it."

c) Thirdly, possessed people often exhibit clairvoyant abilities. This can be quite embarrassing for the counsellors, since it is not unknown for the possessed person to be able to reveal the secret sins of the one counselling him. I was a witness to this once myself.

Ex. 42. A possessed woman was once brought to me in France. Suddenly while we were praying, the woman jumped to her feet, seized the jacket of one of the other ministers present and shouted out, "You hypocrite. Put your own life in order before you try to help others."

d) Finally, possessed people sometimes speak in a language or languages in a state of trance which they had no previous knowledge of. This is, I think, the strongest argument against the theory that these people are only mentally ill. The mentally ill, no matter what they are suffering from, can never speak in a language they have previously not learnt.

Ex. 43. In New Zealand a man told me of how, at a spiritistic meeting he had heard a medium suddenly start speaking in the German language although he knew that the medium himself did not understand the language at all.

Ex. 44. The Brazilian medium Mirabelli was able to speak 25 different foreign languages when in a state of trance.

Ex. 45. The possessed boy in the Philippines, who I have already mentioned, spoke more than ten different languages and dialects, including Russian, in the presence of myself and the other Christian workers who were counselling him. In normal life the boy, however, could only speak pidgin English and one Philippine dialect.

These examples should serve as a warning to all those

who put so much stress on speaking in tongues. There are so many possessed people, spiritistic mediums, and magicians in the world today with an ability to speak in tongues derived from demonic sources rather than from the Holy Spirit, that seeking this gift for ourselves can be a very dangerous occupation.

There is one further striking factor to mention with regard to the counselling of possessed people. If the counsellor is not a born again Christian, one finds that not one of the characteristics we have just mentioned will make an appearance. It is only when a possessed person is confronted by a truly spiritual attitude that he will react, or rather the spirit within him will react with the fury we have already described.

3. Can genuine Christians be possessed?

We come now to a question about which there is a great deal of argument. People seem to divide themselves into two distinct groups. In the English speaking world, Christians usually state quite dogmatically, "No, it's impossible for a Christian to be possessed." From a scriptural point of view this seems to be the correct line to take. However, many missionaries and experienced Christian workers retort, "But we have actually come across cases of possession among believers." These then are the two groups, and their outlooks often clash quite strongly.

I heard in Africa of one particular missionary being sent home because he believed in the possibility of Christians being possessed. But then again I have met another missionary in Africa who had actually been possessed himself for a period of 18 months. He, like many others, had previously believed it impossible for Christians to be possessed. However, his own experience made him change his earlier theological outlook.

I found my several meetings with Dr. Edman, the late

chancellor of Wheaton College, very significant. He told me of the many cases he had personally come across when he had been a missionary in South America, which had finally convinced him in his own mind that Christians could be possessed.

Then again the opinion of Dr. Evans from Wales is also very revealing. He must be getting on well into his nineties now, if he is still alive. I last had the opportunity of speaking to him in 1962. This aged witness of the Lord traces his Christian experience back to the days of the Welsh revival. He too was of the opinion that a Christian guilty of disobedience could be possessed.

In my travels throughout the world, I too have come across a number of instances which seem to bear out this opinion.

Is there then any answer to the problem? We should wonder that there is such a difference of opinion among genuine born again believers. And yet there can only be one truth concerning the matter, and not two. This therefore means that either one or other of the two groups is wrong, or maybe the final answer lies elsewhere and both groups are right in their own way, but are only looking at the problem from different points of view.

One important thing to note, however, is that those who advocate the inflexible doctrine that Christians cannot under any circumstances be possessed, have usually had no experience of possession themselves. On the other hand those who have worked on mission fields where cases of possession have been in evidence, usually side with Dr. Edman and Dr. Evans in believing that Christians can be possessed. The missionary I have just mentioned who up till his own possession had always advocated the dogmatic view, said later, "God taught me a lesson, and cured me of being so inflexible in my ideas."

Although personally I am more inclined to take the side

of those who believe in the possibility of a Christian
being possessed, I sometimes think that there may be
a way of bringing the two sides together. But whatever
the case, in heaven all our quarrelling will cease.

Very briefly though, here are some observations which
should help us to understand the more dogmatic point
of view.

a) Only God knows the heart of man. Perhaps a person
we believe is converted and who seems to be involved in
Christian work, has never in reality experienced the
rebirth.

b) Perhaps we are confusing the two ideas of possession
and obsession. It may be that a Christian we consider to
be possessed, is actually only obsessed, and that instead
of indwelling him, the demons are only surrounding him.

c) It is also a possibility that in order to cure a believer
of pride or arrogance, or hardness of heart, God can
allow him to undergo a temporary period of possession.
This could have been the case with the missionary who
told me his own story of possession.

d) In my own experience I have found that believers
who fall victim to possession do so only temporarily and
are later delivered. Unbelievers on the other hand can
remain possessed all their lives.

e) We can possibly make use of the words of the
apostle Paul in 1 Corinthians 5 : 5, where he speaks of
a believer being delivered up to Satan for the destruction
of the flesh, but his spirit being saved in the day of the
Lord Jesus.

f) We must also not forget that a believer can backslide.
In the New Testament we read of the cases of Hymenaeus,
Alexander and Demas.

Counselling work shows that particularly with believers, possession follows a very contradictory course. I
will quote just two examples of this.

Ex. 46. Some years ago now, a minister brought a

possessed woman to see me. During her attacks she would begin to curse and blaspheme terribly. However, when the attack had passed, she could start to pray very movingly and would feel completely at peace with God. It appeared, therefore, that during her actual attacks the devil was ruling in her life, but that when they had passed the Holy Spirit took over control. An experience like this is very difficult to understand, but we cannot just simply brush it aside because it does not fit into our rigid doctrinal point of view. Yet it was obviously God's will that this kind of double life in the woman should cease. Often when I meet people who completely refuse to bend for one moment from their dogmatic assertion, I feel like confronting them with the plagued people I have been mentioning and saying to them, "All right then, since you know so much and have such a lot of experience in these things, you deliver these people from the bondage they are in."

Ex. 47. In the last century the Rev. Blumhardt had a great deal of experience with regard to the question and problem of possession. The story of his counselling work with the possessed girl Gottliebin Dittus has already been published in Germany. As in the previous example, the girl's moods varied to the extent that one moment she would be raging about, and the next moment she would be clinging to Jesus. As Blumhardt counselled the girl further, he discovered that a great deal of sorcery had been practised in the house in which she lived.

It is a matter of experience that Christians who have lived in houses where either magic or spiritism have been practised, are much more likely to fall prey to possession than other believers. Already on a number of occasions I have been called to visit such houses in order to meet the actual people involved.

Ex. 48. A Bible student in the Philippines had been a Christian for about one year. As I prayed with him, a rough voice called out of him, "He belongs to us. His whole family has belonged to us for more than 300 years." "No," I retorted, "he belongs to the Lord Jesus to whom he's surrendered his life." The voices spoke again, "That's not true. His ancestors have subscribed themselves to us. He is ours by right." The conversation revealed that the ancestors of this unhappy student had not only practised sorcery, but some of them had even subscribed themselves to the devil with their own blood. This was the reason why, in spite of his conversion, the student had become possessed.

In 1 Corinthians 13:9 Paul writes, "For our knowledge is imperfect." It is only in eternity that we will fully understand. Realizing this therefore, we should be very hesitant in condemning a brother whose views differ from ours in certain points. And this is particularly true on the question of possession, for there seem to be sufficient aspects of the problem to enable each to understand the other's point of view. Furthermore there is a definite difference between the possession of believers and the possession of unbelievers. With believers this possessed condition is perhaps only a very severe form of affliction and trial through which they have to temporarily pass.

B. HEALING AND THE SCRIPTURES

I. *The Importance and Meaning of Medicine*

When talking about scriptural forms of healing, one must never overlook the achievements of medicine. God has given us the gift of understanding, and this gift must be developed and used according to his will. I hold medical science in very high esteem, since it is one of the greatest servants of mankind. It is really unnecessary to point out the various achievements of this successful branch of science, since for example, almost the whole world is acquainted with the history of the South African dentist, Dr. Blaiberg, who for almost two years continued living with the help of a transplanted heart. Yes, the era of organ transplants and replacements is upon us.

A young boy with a weak heart beat has lived for a number of years now with an electric pulsator stuck to his chest with elastoplast. The pulsator transmits a continual stream of electrical impulses to his heart in order to keep it beating. An American surgeon has inserted a plastic pump into another patient to actually replace his heart. A German person I know, having lost his arm in the last war, travelled to Moscow quite recently in order to have a new arm sewn on in place of the one he had lost. One can imagine the man's joy in being able to look after himself once more, after having to depend on other people for so long. Today we find that hands and arms, kidneys, hearts, eyes, and even livers and lungs, are being transplanted into people. What a blessing from God this can be to all the crippled people in the world today. We should be very thankful to our Creator for having endowed man with such gifts as He has.

Obviously though, there are a number of questions raised here for the Christian. For example, if after an accident one receives a number of pints of another person's blood, is one's frame of mind affected in any way? Someone will no doubt refer us to the passage in the Bible which reads, "For the life of the body is in the blood" (Lev. 17:11). I believe some Bible students on account of this verse even refuse to undergo blood transfusions. But a similar question arises in the case of heart transplants. Dr. Blaiberg was asked whether or not he had noticed any changes in his thoughts or his emotions. Although his answer was negative, doctors have nevertheless been able to observe a number of psychical changes taking place in other heart transplant patients. However, they put this down to organic reasons. But we could continue to object by saying, "Well, what about the man with the Russian arm? He doesn't know what crimes the arm has previously been guilty of. It could have been the arm of a murderer, or a person who has tortured Christians in prison." I am well aware of all these objections, but it is my conviction that one is able to bring everything to God in prayer. If the circumstances required it, I would personally allow the surgeons to sew another arm on to me, but I would pray at the same time, "O God, will you cleanse and remove the sins this arm has been guilty of, through the blood of your Son." Then, knowing that nothing is to be rejected if it is received with thanksgiving (1 Tim. 4:4, 5), I would use my new arm in the service of God and other people. In the same way, I would feel quite free to allow my body to be used for the benefit of others after my death. The soul of man is in no way effected by the loss of a hand or a foot. Indeed it would even make me happy to think that a blind person was perhaps able to see again through the use of one of my eyes. God is a God of mercy, and it is He we have to thank for having allowed medical science to progress as far as it has done in this present generation. I feel sure that the Christians in Galatia would have been more than willing to pluck out their own eyes, had it been physically possible, in order to help Paul in his work (Gal. 4:15).

II. First Things First

Hans Bruns, who has been a friend of mine for many years, often used to say, "The most important thing is that the most important thing remains the most important thing." Although this slogan can become monotonous, it nevertheless contains a lot of truth. But what is the most important thing? If you ask the man in the street, he is more than likely to answer, "My health, of course."

Thus we find this very thought being expressed in our day-to-day greetings in the form, "How are you?" "Oh, all right, thank you." "Ah, well, that's the most important thing." And yet, when all is said and done, it is not.

We live in a day when materialism is experiencing one of its greatest triumphs. People will sacrifice almost anything to hang on to their own existence. Nothing is too dear to pay when it comes to the question of preserving a person's health — and so the most important thing is completely forgotten: one's personal relationship with God.

By reading the story of the paralytic in Mark 2, we can see what the true order of priority really is. The first thing that Jesus said to the man was, "My son, your sins are forgiven." It was only later that he turned to the man and said, "I say to you, rise, take up your pallet and go home."

We must remember then, that the most important problem facing us is not the health of our bodies but rather the forgiveness of our sins. We find the same emphasis in James 5:14–19, where confession of sin is recommended whenever healing of the body is sought.

Any healing movement which is not at the same time a movement of repentance, will wander into error. When revival first broke out in Indonesia, there was a continual danger of this actually happening, until in 1965 God sent the German missionary Detmar Scheunemann to the area, to guide the healing movement into scriptural pathways.

Sometimes God takes it upon himself to personally teach us this vital lesson, that forgiveness is of more importance than healing. To illustrate this I can quote three short examples.

Ex. 49. A farmer's wife lay in bed on the point of death. Wanting to confess her sins to another Christian before she died, she wondered to whom to turn. She was reluctant to ask the local minister to come to her bedside, for she felt there was something amiss with his faith. It was then that God stepped in by sending another Christian man into the neighbourhood. He had just come to spend a short holiday in the district. When the woman heard of his arrival, she sent a message to him, asking him to come and visit her. He came, and during a period lasting two hours, the woman made an open confession of her sins. She was now prepared to die. However, events proved otherwise. Later when the Christian brother visited the farm again, he found the farmer's wife standing in the yard with a look of joy on her face. He could hardly believe his eyes. What had happened? It transpired that after she had confessed her sins, in addition to forgiving her, the Lord had also touched her body and healed her. Yet at the time of her confession the thought of healing had never really entered her mind.

Ex. 50. A woman came to see me once when I was in South Africa. She told me that she was suffering from cancer and advanced metastasis and had only a short time to live. Because of this she wanted to make a full confession of her sins before she died. In spite of the fact that her visit to me had no connection with any desire for healing on her own part, I felt constrained to pray that the Lord would in fact heal her body as well as forgive her sins. For this reason I asked another Christian brother to join me and together we prayed for her under the laying on of hands according to James 5:14. Having to leave the country shortly after this, I heard nothing more about the woman until a year and a half later. It was then that the brother with whom I had prayed wrote and told me that instead of dying the woman had been cured by the Lord and was now better. This was another case in which healing had followed the forgiveness of sins. Let me say very quickly though, that I personally do not possess the gift of healing. That I am privileged to experience events of this nature in the course of my Christian service, is only the result of the Lord's desire to glorify his own name in the life of some suffering person.

Just before writing this book I came across a completely new example illustrating the same principle.

Ex. 51. About eight years ago an active charmer came to me to be counselled. As we knelt together in the vestry of a church, he confessed his sins aloud before God, calling upon him for forgiveness. I have seldom if ever in my life, heard a man pray so earnestly and movingly. After our time together, the Lord answered his prayer and delivered him. I never saw the man again until a few days ago when he visited me at my house. At first I did not even recognize him after all these years. He told me that the Lord had continued to keep him, but in the course of our conversation another side to the story came to the surface. When he had visited me the first time, he had been suffering from tuberculosis of both lungs and his health had been rapidly deteriorating. However, after his confession and conversion, the disease had come to a standstill. The cure had lasted. Now for the first time I was able to hear the whole story. We can only utter praise to God for being so merciful. At the time of his confession the man had made no mention of his illness at all. He had come solely on account of his terrible feeling of guilt before God. The Lord had forgiven him — and healed him! Hallelujah!

In the Scriptures the order is always: the soul's welfare, then that of the body. In the sermon on the mount Jesus even went so far as to say, "If your right eye causes you to sin, pluck it out. If your right hand causes you to sin, cut it off." It is better to enter the kingdom of heaven with only one eye or only one arm than to be thrown into hell with a healthy body. Whether we are crippled for life or suffering from an incurable illness, we can still experience the glory of God in our lives. Our aim there-

fore must not be to hang on to our health at all costs.
We should realize that the presence of the Lord, the power
of his Word, and the promise of the Holy Spirit are of
far more importance than a healthy body. Our principle
concern should be that of fulfilling the will of God in our
own lives, and not the satisfying of our own desires.
Even in a state of illness one can be mightily used of God.
So then, forgiveness is essential, healing a possibility.

III. *Jesus, Physician of the Incurable*

The last thing we want to do in writing a chapter on
scriptural healing is to sensationalize healing as such.
Our sole aim is to bring glory to the name of the Lord
Jesus. One finds sometimes that it is often better not to
publicize stories of God's healing power if one wants to
prevent damage being done to His work. However, since
in the process of warning people we have had to quote
a number of negative examples on the subject of the
demonic, in order to present a balanced picture it is very
necessary to take time to describe the positive side as
well. And if we failed to do this, it might appear to some
that the devil was alone successful in this area.

However, if I personally had not known that the victory was truly Christ's, this book would never have been
written. For many years now the victorious song written
by the Rev. Blumhardt has been my motto: That Jesus has
won is decided for ever, the whole world belongs to him.

It is to the victory of Christ over all the powers of
disease and darkness that the following examples testify.
And again let me repeat that the examples concern either
people I know or mission fields I have visited.

Ex. 52. First of all then a story from England. It is
encouraging to find that although this land is filled with
spiritual healers and unscriptural extremists, there are
still many truly sound born again Christians there too.
A Baptist minister invited me to hold a series of five

meetings in his church. While I was staying with him, he told me his wife's medical history. Two years previously she had had an operation against cancer. However, the cancer had continued to spread and her larynx had become affected, so much so that she had lost the use of her vocal cords. Finally the cancer had reached her brain and she had fallen into a coma. To the husband's dismay the doctor told him that his wife's condition was hopeless. After being in a coma for four weeks though, his wife had suddenly regained consciousness for a short while. During this time, she had asked her husband to bring two elders of their church to her bedside to pray for her and to lay hands upon her according to James 5. This the minister had done, and they had prayed for his wife under the laying on of hands. There had been an immediate change in her condition. She regained consciousness, her voice returned and she recovered. I was actually able to meet her for myself and talk to her in their own home. She was full of life and in good health. Neither the minister nor his wife had had anything to do with the Pentecostal movement. It was merely a case of Jesus glorifying his own name. Jesus is the only one to whom we can turn for help.

Ex. 53. When in Nigeria, I was able to visit a number of the mission stations among the Ibos in the area which is today called Biafra. One tribe I came into particular contact with, was the Izi tribe. While I was with them, I was privileged to be told about a glorious instance of the healing of one of the native pastors. The pastor had been suffering from a serious disease of the lungs and had been almost on the point of dying. X-rays had shown that both his lungs were filled with blood and the doctors expected him to die in a matter of days. They said he was literally drowning in his own blood. It was then that the pastor had asked the missionary who was telling me the story to come and see him. "I sense I am not going to die," he told the missionary. "It seems to me as if this is only an attack of the powers of darkness. Please, will you command these powers to leave me." The missionary, however, hesitated for he was more inclined to believe what the doctors had told him than to believe what his native brother said. But the pastor urged him again. Finally he agreed and he prayed roughly with the words, "Lord Jesus, if my brother here is right, and this is only an attack of the enemy, then deliver him. But forgive me if what I am saying is silly." The missionary then commanded the evil powers to go, although in his heart he doubted if he was doing the right thing. What happened? Suddenly the pastor vomitted and brought up a vast amount of blood. The doctor was called immediately, but he said that this was the end. Yet instead of dying, the man began to recover. A few days later he was X-rayed again. A miracle had taken place. The massive caverns in his lungs had closed up, and instead of certain death, the native Christian was wonderfully healed by the hand of the Lord.

Events of this nature are nothing we can copy. God cannot be forced to do the same for all who are suffering in this way. He alone is sovereign. It is he, and not us, who decides who is to be healed and who is not. And above all, we must never fall into the trap of believing that just because God has acted in this way once, we can now start commanding the powers of darkness at the bedside of every sick person, as is frequently the habit of members of certain extreme sects.

Ex. 54. Sometimes mental illness can be as complicated, and often even more so, than organic disease. To illustrate this fact, let me quote another example from Nigeria. A woman missionary started developing a form of religious compulsion neurosis. Whenever she wanted to go to sleep, she would suddenly hear a voice within her saying, "Get up and pray." Thinking the voice to be that of her

Lord, she would start to pray. However, hardly had she finished and settled down in bed again than she would again be commanded, "Get up and read your Bible." And so it went on. The commands were so numerous that she was prevented from getting almost any rest. Her waking hours were similarly plagued with the same thoughts and impulses. In the end she started to suffer from blasphemous thoughts as well. Some other missionaries and friends visited her and prayed for her, but the missionary doctor said that she would have to be admitted to the hospital. However, one of the missionaries had the impression that something was very strange with the whole affair. He suspected a demonic attack, especially since a lot of sorcery was practised in this particular area. Not daring to speak about this to the woman herself, he finally prayed, "Lord, I'm not absolutely sure what is wrong with our sister, but you know. So if she is being plagued by the devil, then please deliver her." He then commanded the demons in the name of the Lord to leave the woman alone. The woman suddenly jerked and acted as if she were being sick. That night she was able to sleep peacefully and without disturbance for the first time in a long while. Her compulsion neurosis never returned. She had been cured.

This is yet another instance when the Lord has personally stepped in and healed a person, but again, it must not be made into a blueprint. Many compulsion neuroses have no connection with the demonic, so let us beware of hasty conclusions. But on the other hand I must admit for the sake of fairness that many compulsion neuroses I have come across over the years have been the direct result of sins of sorcery. And it need not always be the victim's own sins of sorcery. One can be burdened through inheriting the punishment of one's ancestors sins, or merely by living in a neighbourhood where a lot of occultism is practised as was true in the last example.

But running through the stories we have just been mentioning is the sound of victory. The One who died for us on the cross is equal to every situation. All power belongs to Him. For this reason we should not shrink back from following Him at whose name the whole world will one day be compelled to bow.

Since miracles of healing and their accompanying phenomena often tend to lead into unscriptural pathways, we must again stress the following fact. In the majority of cases confession and forgiveness are the basic conditions determining whether God will act in any further way on behalf of a person who is physically or mentally ill. Only very occasionally will the Lord step in and heal an unbeliever, although I know of one or two cases where this has in fact happened.

Ex. 55. A Moslem in Malaysia because he was very ill went to the Christians to ask them if they could help him. His own Moslem priest had been unable to do anything for him. The Christians at first spoke to him about Jesus and then prayed for him. God listened to the prayers of his children and the Moslem was healed. When the Christians saw the man again, they begged him saying, "Jesus has healed you. Please, you must try and follow him." To this the Moslem replied, "I can't accept Jesus. I only came to you to be healed." As a result of this his illness returned and later attempts to heal him through prayer failed.

Jesus is not to be taken lightly by anyone. And we must not forget that these examples occur in an atmosphere much closer to that of the early Church than the atmosphere found in the tired and decrepit Christendom of the West.

IV. *The Glory of Suffering*

Suffering and disease are representative of many classes in God's school. For example:

1. Suffering can be a form of punishment. A person who is unprepared to be guided by the goodness of God may sometimes feel the rod of his anger.

In a similar way a person who has become lost in the toil and rush of life, giving little thought to the state of his own soul, may sometimes be led by God into the quietness of a hospital ward where he will have time to rediscover both himself and God.

2. Suffering can also be God's way of teaching us a lesson. Many a self-assured person has stormed through life with the conviction that he is well able to manage his own affairs, until God has stepped in with a halt sign designed to bring him to his senses.

Sometimes to cure us of our coldness and lack of understanding towards those who are ill, God will simply break us. I know of an old evangelist who had never had a day's illness in all his life. It was a well-known fact that he had a very hard attitude towards people who were sick. Then one day God caught him in an avalanche in order to teach him something about His mercy.

3. Then suffering can be a means of preservation. One wonders how many sudden illnesses have really been a blessing in disguise. Only the Lord knows what great disasters he has spared us from in this manner.

4. Suffering can also lead one into greater maturity. Diamonds are only produced under great pressure, but even then they are still not the precious stones we are familiar with. They must first be carefully polished by the master's hand, before they finally become the costly jewels we prize so much.

5. Finally, suffering can be a school of holiness. For me one of the most moving and at the same time most

blessed experiences of my life was when I sat at the bedside of a dear 78-year-old Christian lady. Here briefly is her story.

Ex. 56. As a young girl she had once been engaged. She was already a Christian at the time. Then through being confined to bed on account of a severe illness, her engagement had been broken off. Since she had only been working for a few years, her insurance company soon refused to pay for the mounting doctor's fees. However, because her condition was so grave, she had to be admitted to a hospital. But who was to pay? It transpired that both the senior surgeon and the medical superintendent of the hospital were men who really cared, and instead of clinging to the letter of the law as the insurance company had done, they allowed the woman to remain in the hospital quietly receiving treatment, although there was no one to foot the bill. How long did this go on for? Four months? No. Four years then? No — the answer is almost unbelievable. For forty years the woman remained in the hospital receiving her treatment free through the mercy of those who continually cared for her. How grateful we ought to be for people like this.

But later the senior post in the hospital fell to another doctor. When he visited the now aging woman he started reckoning: 365 days of medical treatment each year. Doctors fees and laboratory costs. Medicines. This is too much. "Haven't you got any relations?" he asked her. "No," she replied. "Then what about some friends?" "Yes, I have friends," was the answer. "Good," retorted the doctor, "tell your friends that someone must come and fetch you. You can't stay here any longer."

The next night the patient hardly slept at all. "O Lord," she begged, "You are the only one I have. Haven't you a place for me? Why don't you come and take me home?"

In the end some friends fetched her and as an expression of great Christian love took her into their own home.

It was in the house of this Christian family that I first met this paralysed saint. "How long have you been like this?" I wanted to know. "For 54 years," came the reply. It was exactly the same number of years as the years of my life.

Yet I was amazed as I sat beside her bed. There was not one word of complaint to be heard. Here was someone who really knew how to pray, and through bearing the marks of suffering, she was at the same time being prepared for the glory that is to be hers in heaven. Already in her little room as she lay in bed the glory of God shone out of her. Never in my life have I witnessed the likes of this. Instead of I counselling her, it was she who counselled me, and I who was blessed. How pale and insignificant the life of a busy Christian worker appears before the presence of this humble child of God. And even as I write these words, her life of quiet service for the Lord continues. Dear reader, have you some moments to set aside for this sister as she lies on her bed of sickness? And then have you enough time to thank God for the health with which he has blessed you?

Humanly speaking one would say that life had passed this woman by. A broken engagement, the loss of her health, no means of livelihood, a paralysed body, and now a lifetime confined to bed. Yet the very glory of God rests over her life, the glory of the One who collapsed under the weight of his cross; the glory of the One whose hands and feet were pierced with nails.

Is not the glory radiating from the life of this dear sister far greater than the glory revealed in a hundred cases of miraculous healing? One wonders how many blessings we lose and how much glory passes us by, when our continual thought is to pray every trial away. To be in tune with the will of God is far better than continually calling on him for healing, yet in his mercy God still hears us, for his steadfast love endures for ever.

C. DELIVERANCE AND THE SCRIPTURES

I. *The Qualifications of the Counsellor*

1. The victory of the name of Jesus.

It would be utterly impossible to do any form of counselling work among the occultly oppressed if it were not for the fact that Jesus had overcome the powers of darkness on the cross. Paul writes triumphantly in Colossians 2:15, "Christ has disarmed the principalities and powers and made a public example of them, triumphing over them in his cross."

In view of this fact one can adopt one of three attitudes.

a) The first is to refuse to take the victory of Christ seriously. Those who adopt this attitude are for ever tortured by a fear of evil spirits and the demonic.

b) As opposed to this, some people go to the opposite extreme. They say, "Christ has settled the matter for us. It's therefore no concern of ours any more." And millions of people thereby remain in their fetters unable to get free.

The error into which this second group falls can be seen by considering the following. If Christ has borne our diseases in a literal sense, then disease does not exist any more. If Christ has overcome death, then no one need die any more. But doctrines like this lead nowhere. This theological attitude is almost on the same level as the idea: a Christian can never be obsessed or possessed.

c) The third attitude one can adopt is to acknowledge the victory of Christ, but at the same time to realize that Satan still puts up a bitter 'rear-guard action' against us. Christians must ever be careful of going to extremes. Our aim must neither be too high nor too low.

We must recognize the battle. We must recognize the

enemy. But far more important, we must recognize the Saviour who has obtained the victory for us.

Ex. 57. I was once the guest of Dr. Eitel in Japan. He had formerly been a missionary in China. One day he had been called to visit a woman who was ill. When he arrived at the farm belonging to the family, he found that the Taoist priest was already there and was about to sacrifice a chicken and use the blood to drive the evil spirits away. As Dr. Eitel went to enter the house, a woman with a wild expression on her face and with her hair hanging loose sprang at him. There was no time at all in which to pray. He could only cry out, "Jesus saves." With this the woman collapsed on the floor. The battle was over. The power of the name of Jesus had overcome.

Ex. 58. A woman missionary in New Guinea, on arriving at a village she had never visited before, called at the large house at the entrance of the village, little realizing it was the house of the chief witchdoctor. As she entered, she saw a man crouch down on the floor and give her a terrible look. The missionary sensed at once there were evil powers emanating from the man. She immediately started to pray that Christ would protect her. A spiritual duel developed. In the end she was able to call out, "Jesus saves." The witchdoctor jerked, and then collapsed on the floor. The battle was over.

> Jesus, the name high over all,
> In hell, or earth, or sky:
> Angels and men before it fall,
> And devils fear and fly.
> Jesus the prisoner's fetters breaks,
> And bruises Satan's head;
> Power into strengthless souls He speaks,
> And life into the dead.

2. The counsellor's commission and equipment.

The apostle James writes (3:1), "Let not many of you become teachers." A statement like this applies even more so in the area of the occult. No one should ever rush into this work. It is better to wait for God to bring the occultly oppressed to us, than to go out looking for them ourselves.

In order to counsel such people, a Christian needs a commission from God and the equipment provided for him by the Holy Spirit.

Ex. 59. A friend of mine, a Christian doctor, after reading my book 'Christian Counselling and Occultism' decided to take up this sort of work. He therefore began to counsel people oppressed by occultism. After a year he lost his reason and was later discovered wandering around in a forest mentally ill.

Ex. 60. During one of my visits to Japan, Dr. Carrol, a missionary working there, told me the story of a young Christian worker. Without any experience behind him, the young man had gone to a heathen temple to try and drive the evil spiritual atmosphere away from the place. He commanded the spirits in the name of Jesus, but the result was that his own life went to pieces. His fellow missionaries had to send him to a mental hospital.

Ex. 61. Another missionary, although just as inexperienced, rented a house opposite a Shinto shrine. He felt he had to pray for the people who visited and worshipped at the shrine. However, he too lost his reason and started suffering from fits of rage. He had to be sent back from Japan to America in a straight-jacket.

Without a commission from God, a Christian should not venture too far into the area of the demonic and the occult. There are certain rules that have to be obeyed.

People with a sensitive nervous system or maybe with an occult oppression of their own should never attempt to do any work in this field. Recent converts and young women should also refrain from this type of work. It is obviously another matter though, if there are no experienced Christian men at hand to help. In a case like this women and sometimes even girls have to be thrown into the front line.

An absolutely essential part of the equipment is a definite experience of conversion and rebirth through the power of the Holy Spirit, together with an extensive prayer life. One must also continually call upon the Lord to give us spiritual authority in these matters. In Luke 9:1—2 we find the story of how Jesus imparted a threefold authority to his disciples, and this included the authority over demons. A Christian working in this field of counselling must also live soberly and have his life founded upon the teachings of the Bible. Fanatics, extremists, psychical tongues speakers, and occult neurotics are unfit for this type of work. I know a comment like this will raise a lot of dust. But why should the truth be concealed? The tongues speakers of today — not the apostles — are people with nervous dispositions, unsuited for the testing battle. The value of some form of medical training has already been mentioned.

II. *Counselling Procedure*

In the following paragraphs we shall be seeking to give a systematic picture of the counselling of the occultly oppressed. For this reason a person may draw the false conclusion that there is some kind of pattern or stereotyped method involved. But this is not true. The Holy Spirit needs no pattern. He is able to sweep away in an instant all our considerations and give immediate help. I have actually witnessed this myself once.

Ex. 62. While I was speaking in Auckland, New Zealand, a missionary came and visited me. "Do you recognize me?" he asked. No, I said I did not. He went on, "Six years ago you were in Australia. I wanted to talk to you, but you had to pack your bags in order to catch the aeroplane. However, while you were packing, you listened to my occult history. You only had a little time in which to pray with me. But ever since then I have been delivered." The Holy Spirit had stepped in, for He had recognized there had been no time for a long conversation.

We should never start imagining therefore that the Lord has need of our often complicated counselling procedures.

Many years of experience have shown me that deliverances of this nature are extremely rare. For this reason we must pay special attention to all that the Scriptures offer us concerning the help of the occultly oppressed. Sometimes the battle for deliverance takes not minutes, nor just a few hours, but years.

1. Deliverance is possible only through Christ

Ex. 63. A student suffering from depressions and lacking all desire to go on living, once sat in front of me. I tried to show him the way to Christ. He was neither able nor willing to take this step. He therefore found no relief for his depressions either.

Jesus said in Matthew 11:28, "deute pros me, pantes hoi kopiontes kai pephortismenoi" — "Come to me all the wearied and the burdened." Come to me. Whoever fails to obey this call must remain the victim of his occult bondage.

Ex. 64. A young woman came to me after a meeting and I counselled her in the vestry of the church. "I'm burdened just like you described in your talk," she said. "Can you help me to get out of this?" "How do you stand in relation to Jesus?" I asked her. She became angry. "Look, I want to get well. Don't start talking to me about your Jesus." She left the vestry excitedly. There was nothing I could do to help her.

In the case of occult subjection neither psychology, depth-psychology, nor psychiatry can be of any help. Autosuggestion, meditation and yoga are likewise impotent. And nothing can be gained by turning to Buddhism, Hinduism, or the Moslem faith.

The only source of help in this world is Jesus.

If a person is unwilling to come to him, he will go away sorrowful like the rich young ruler who was also not prepared to do as Jesus told him. In the Acts of the Apostles it is written, "There is salvation in no one else, for there is no other name under heaven given among men by which we must be saved." And that name is Jesus.

2. Every object of sorcery must be destroyed.

In the great revival which Paul experienced in Ephesus many of those who were now believers brought their books on magic arts together and burned them in the sight of all (Acts 19:19).

In the revival in Indonesia the natives brought their fetishes and occult objects together in heaps and destroyed them in a similar way.

Magical books and occult objects carry with them a hidden ban. Anyone not prepared to rid himself of this ban will be unable to free himself from the influence of the powers of darkness.

Ex. 65. A young man wanted to surrender his life to Christ. In spite of burning his books on spiritism though, he was not delivered. Some Christian brothers continued to pray for him but there was still no change. Then two of them visited the young man's home. There on the bookshelf they found a leather bound copy of one of Jakob Lorber's spiritistical books. The young man did not want to part with the book with its gold embossed cover and gilt-edges. However, when he did finally burn it, he was completely delivered.

During various evangelistic campaigns numerous people have handed letters of protection, letters of good omen, threatening letters, and copies of the 6th and 7th Book of Moses to me. I always throw them into the fire. Some naive people, however, hang on to these things, especially when they find Bible verses contained within them.

Ex. 66. In Port Elizabeth, South Africa, the Rev. Petersen told me the following story. "One of my congregation reads his Bible, prays and has a real desire to follow Jesus but somehow just can't get through. At home he's got some of the writings of the Rosecrucians and he simply won't part with them. They therefore prevent him from making a clear-cut decision."

Ex. 67. A girl from Manchester immigrated to South Africa. She became engaged to a young man there who practised black magic. Once when she came home to Manchester for a holiday, strange ghostlike phenomena started occurring at her parent's house. The rooms would fill with smoke although there were no fires lit and there was often a penetrating smell of decaying bodies in every room. The family sought the advice of an Anglican minister. He advised them to destroy anything the girl had received from her fiancé and encouraged her to break off the engagement. She did so and afterwards the haunting ceased. The girl's mother was a Christian and had prayed a lot that God would deliver them all.

Ex. 68. A missionary in South Africa entered the house of a Hindu family. The daughter immediately started sliding about on the floor as if she were a snake. She just could not control herself. Her parents had no power over her either. The missionary asked them, "Have you any idols in the house? If you have, then get rid of them at once." They followed his advice. The missionary then prayed for the afflicted girl and she was set free.

Sometimes when one asks a person to destroy his occult objects, one meets with a lot of resistance, especially if the articles are also extremely expensive works of art. Yet even the little figures made out of precious stones which often originate from heathen temples have to be destroyed if the owner finds he cannot free himself from his occult oppression.

And this brings us to an important point. Some missionaries are actually enthusiastic collectors of devil's masks and similar objects of heathen ritual worship. Through hanging the trophies up in their homes they burden the whole house and all who live in it. If one points to the dangers involved, they usually just laugh. A professor of theology in South Africa called me a backwoodsman when I told him he ought to remove the figureens from his house that had been used as idols. These idols have sometimes been used for years or even decades in heathen rituals. In this way they become crystallization points for demonic powers in houses where they are displayed as works of art. The Spirit of God does not dwell with idols, even in a so-called Christian home.

Whoever is not prepared to forsake his occult books and objects need expect no deliverance.

A similar problem occasionally arises when magicians or spiritists living in a small village donate perhaps a carpet, or a chalice, or some hanging, to the local church in order to gain a name for themselves. I am convinced that gifts of this nature should never be used in churches. I once said as much in a church near Hanover when the minister showed me the pulpit cloth and added, "We were given this by a well-known spiritist who subsequently committed suicide." I replied, "I would not have the freedom to preach from a pulpit decorated with a spiritistic gift. What has Christ got to do with Baal?"

3. Mediumistic contacts and friendship must be broken.

This brings us to a very complicated problem. An example will best illustrate what I mean.

Ex. 69. A young girl was spiritually awakened during an evangelistic campaign. She wanted to become a Christian. While she was being counselled, it was discovered that her mother was a card-layer and was still actively engaged in the terrible art of fortune-telling. The counsellor was now faced with the problem of whether the daughter would ever be able to find any inner peace in these circumstances. There was no question of the daughter not abhorring the dreadful practices of her mother, but the evil powers which dwelt in her parent's house would surely make her life into hell if she tried to follow Jesus. If a person has had no experience in counselling work of this nature, he will be unable to understand the advice I finally gave the girl. I told her that somehow she should get a job that took her away from home, and if possible only visit her mother very occasionally. The girl found it difficult to appreciate the advice, yet the result was soon evident. However, the girl started praying for her mother. Each time she did so though, she would be terribly attacked. One should not be surprised at this for the powers of darkness are for ever trying to strike back. I therefore told the girl that she had better stop praying for her mother until her own Christian life had been built up more. She would then be able to form a prayer group that would be able to pray for her mother's deliverance.

Sometimes I advise the children of spiritistic families not to pray for their parents at all if they are still engaged in occult practices. Before all else we must obey the words of Scripture, "Save yourselves from this crooked generation." This is not a form of pious egotism. I cannot hope to help others spiritually, until I myself have been saved. Inexperienced counsellors, however, will be unable to appreciate decisions of this nature, for they will have little knowledge of the terrible attacks which can be levelled by the powers of darkness.

Ex. 70. A married couple in Wellington, New Zealand, came and asked me for some advice. They had been attending some spiritistic meetings for a number of years and had even had their children baptised by the spiritists. But now they both wanted to follow Jesus. I begged them to break off all their friendships with the spiritists they had known and to destroy any books or articles they had obtained from the spiritistic circle (2 Cor. 6:14).

Although many Christians will accept the fact that they must break off relationships with spiritistic friends, there is another area in which one can meet with the greatest misunderstanding. Within certain fanatical and extreme religious groups one finds mediumistic influences and contacts which must also be renounced if one hopes to arrive at any form of inner peace.

I approach this area only with a great deal of reluctance, although I have been able to collect a good deal of information on the subject from all over the world. First an example.

Ex. 71. Bakth Singh is probably being used by God more than any other Indian today. He is for India what Billy Graham is for the USA. Together with him I once visited a Christian conference. During a time of open prayer, someone suddenly began to pray in tongues. But there was no one to interpret. This in itself should have been enough to stop the person speaking in tongues (1 Cor. 14:28). I was personally unhappy with this prayer. After the meeting I asked Bakth Singh, "What did you think about the person who prayed in tongues?" His reply was very revealing: "I asked the Lord to stop the girl from speaking, as I felt it wasn't of the Holy Spirit."

Ex. 72. Peter Octavian is an evangelist being greatly

used by God in the revival in Indonesia. When he visited Stuttgart, we worked together there. On account of the 3,000 people present in the evening, the meeting overflowed into two other halls. At the end of his talk Peter Octavian called upon the people to accept the Lord Jesus as their saviour. He waited quietly for maybe one or two minutes. Suddenly a man on the rostrum began to speak in tongues. I wondered how Peter Octavian would react to this. "In the name of the Lord Jesus," he began, "I command this man to be quiet." He could not have spoken more plainly. Afterwards I asked, "Why did you stop the man?" He replied, "It was clear to me that the enemy was trying to disturb the meeting."

In the Corinthian church speaking in tongues was the gift of the Holy Spirit. Yet the apostle Paul already found it a problem, for a great deal of confusion had already arisen in the church there. The devil, it should be realized, is ever trying to imitate and forge the works of God.

The phenomena which accompany today's new tongues movement as it spreads all over the world indicate it is actually a psychical epidemic, and in many places even a mediumistic movement. Many genuine Christians have had their Christian lives ruined through falling into this mediumistic stream.

Ex. 73. When I was speaking near Leicester in England, a young man came to me and told me his spiritual history. Two years previously he and a friend had decided to secretly pray for the gift of tongues since so many of their other Christian friends were already caught up in the tongues movement. They prayed earnestly for this gift until one day they felt something hot come over them. It was just as if a strange power was overwhelming them. They thought they were experiencing a baptism of the Holy Spirit and afterwards found that they were able to speak in tongues. For some weeks and months they revelled in their new experience, but then came the

great disillusionment. Their 'gifts of tongues' disappeared
and they were filled with a terrible feeling of emptiness.
The young man went on to say, "I not only lost the gift
of tongues, but I also lost my assurance of salvation and
all desire to read the Bible and to pray. I realized myself
that something must be wrong and I became so convinced
of this that I finally renounced my experience of speaking
in tongues and repented, asking God to forgive me. It
was only then that I felt at peace with God once more."
His friend, however, who had prayed together with him
for the gift of tongues, never renounced his experience.
Instead he lost his faith completely and returned to the
world.

This is not just an isolated example, but one of many.
The tongues movement which extremists claim to be a
twentieth century revival movement, is really only a
suggestive epidemic, and Christians must renounce all
contact with it if they hope to keep their own spiritual
lives intact.

The way of truth is very narrow. I ask my readers
therefore not to misunderstand me for apparently only
quoting negative examples. Let me say that I do indeed
know of Christians who in all humility and sometimes
for more than forty years have spoken to their Lord
secretly in an unknown tongue. They make no show
of their gift and have no desire to lead others into their
own experience. They are also sacrificial in their giving,
faithful in their prayers, and above all practise the greatest of Christian virtues which is love. There is nothing
within me which wants to question the genuineness of
their experience. A person who really wants to, will be
able to understand what I am saying. These wonderful
experiences of secret prayer and worship, however, when
compared with the spurious examples associated with the
'tongues movement' occur perhaps only once in every
thousand cases. But there is another misunderstanding

connected with tongues speaking, namely, that one is supposedly only able to worship the Lord truly when speaking or praying 'in a tongue'. Yet this is just not true, since by far the majority of Christians worship God in 'spirit and in truth' without possessing the gift of tongues. Instead they use a tongue that has been cleansed by the blood of the Lord Jesus himself.

We should never forget that such well-known men of God as for example Finney, Wesley, Moody, Spurgeon, Hudson Taylor, Dr. Torrey, Graham Scroggie, F.B. Meyer, and Oswald Chambers, not only did not possess the gift of tongues themselves but were frequently inclined to reject the whole idea of the modern tongues movement. F. B. Meyer, Oswald Chambers, and Graham Scroggie in particular, were against the movement almost from the very start.

The Bible gives us an excellent testing stone to see whether the life of a person who speaks in tongues is scripturally in tune. In 1 Corinthians 14 we find the question of tongues speaking dealt with in great detail. Yet the aim and object of the whole chapter is made plain in the very first verse. There we find the words, "Make love your aim, and earnestly desire the spiritual gifts, especially that you may prophesy." The tendency among tongues speakers, however, is to interpret the whole chapter as if speaking in tongues were the most important thing the apostle was talking about. But to adopt this attitude is to twist the Word of God and to wander into extremism. Paul is actually saying that the gift of prophecy is greater than the gift of tongues. But again there is a vast difference between the gift of prophecy and the ability to tell fortunes. The scriptural 'propheteuein' — the gift of prophecy — is the authoritative gift of forth-telling the messages of God, and not the mediumistic ability of fore-telling the future.

Let us never forget — neither the spirit of extremism

nor the spirit of fortune-telling bear any relationship to
the Holy Spirit of God.

4. Confession

As we leave behind the activities and the exaggerations
of the extremists and enter the domain of repentance and
conversion, and thereby the salvation of mankind, we
find ourselves once more surrounded by the pure and
clear atmosphere of the Scriptures. A person can again
breathe freely when he finds himself in such a sober and
healthy environment.

Generally speaking in most forms of counselling work
confession is usually made in the presence of the counsellor. However, I know of people who have only had God
as their witness when they have made confession of their
sins. There is no law to be made about the matter. God is
able to justify a person no matter how he confesses his
sins, yet personally speaking I usually encourage a person
to follow the advice of James 5:16.

In the case of occult subjection, however, the circumstances are very different. As we have already seen, the
word occult means hidden or secret. The converse of this
is therefore to reveal, or to bring into the light. Thus in
order to reveal the hidden occult sins of a person, confession must usually be made in the presence of a mature
Christian counsellor.

Occultly oppressed people should in fact make an open
confession of every single hidden thing in their lives in
order to remove the very last foothold of the enemy.

Ex. 74. In Suwa on the Fiji Islands a young woman
came to me and confessed that for two years she had
been suffering from attacks of paralysis. The doctors had
been unable to find any cause for her illness. I told the
young woman that I had experienced conditions like hers
before in people whose parents or grandparents had
practised spiritism or crude forms of hypnosis and other

occult practices. I asked her if any of her family had engaged in anything like this. Her reply was negative. I could get no further in counselling her. Later I heard that on the way home she had told the woman with her, that as a young girl she had taken part in some table-lifting. This was undoubtedly the cause of her trancelike states of paralysis.

The confession of a subjected person should not only cover the occult, but also every other department of his life. Yet compulsion must never be used. Unless the confession is completely voluntary, it will be worthless.

The power behind the revival in Uganda in Africa consists in what is called 'walking in the light'. This expression is used by the Christians to describe an almost daily practice of James 5:16. Every hidden resentment and sin is brought into the light. Nothing is allowed to build up or develop which might give an opportunity to the devil.

5. The prayer of renunciation.

In the normal way the thing that follows confession is absolution — the promise of the forgiveness of sins. In my counselling work among the occultly oppressed, however, I have found that I have had to abandon this sequence since the subjected person usually finds it impossible to grasp the fact that his sins have been forgiven. He is simply unable to believe. A barrier seems to lie in his way. I therefore always encourage the victim of occultism to pray a prayer of renunciation first of all.

What do we understand by a prayer of renunciation? In the first century candidates for baptism were asked, "Do you renounce the devil and all his works?" The candidate would answer, "Yes, I renounce the devil and all his works." After this he was baptised. In Latin this prayer is called abrenuntiatia diaboli. Many Christian churches still have similar renunciation formulae in their baptismal or confirmation liturgies. Obviously though a 'formula' or 'liturgical piece' is of no use in the spiritual realm.

In counselling the occultly oppressed, a prayer of renunciation is, however, of great significance. The question is why? Every sin connected with sorcery is basically a contract with the powers of darkness. By means of sorcery the archenemy of mankind gains the right of ownership over a person's life. The same is true even if it is only the sins of a person's parents or grandparents that are involved. The devil is well acquainted with the second commandment which ends, "for I the Lord your God am a jealous God, visiting the iniquity of the fathers upon the children to the third and the fourth generation of those who hate me." The powers of darkness continue to claim their right of ownership although quite often the descendants remain completely unaware of the fact, perhaps since they have had no contact with sorcery themselves. Nevertheless immediately a person in this situation is converted, Satan very soon makes his claim felt.

In praying a prayer of renunciation a person cancels Satan's right both officially and judicially. The counsellor and any other Christian brothers present act as witnesses to this annulment of ownership.

Although modern theologians ridicule the whole idea, the devil is in earnest. Hundreds of examples could be quoted to show just how seriously he takes the matter.

When the occult oppression is minimal, the person who has made his confession will have little difficulty in repeating a prayer of renunciation after the counsellor. The prayer can take the form, "In the name of Jesus I renounce all the works of the devil together with the occult practices of my forefathers, and I subscribe myself to the Lord Jesus Christ, my Lord and Saviour, both now and for ever. In the name of the Father, and of the Son, and of the Holy Spirit, amen."

✓The prayer is not a formula. Every time it is prayed, it can take a different form.

In severe cases of oppression on the other hand a number of complications can arise when it comes to praying a prayer of renunciation.

Ex. 75. In Switzerland the son of a bishop came to see me. It soon became evident what the root cause of his trouble was. When I asked him to pray a prayer of renunciation after me, he found he could not bring his hands together to pray. His mouth would not open either. He just ground his teeth and was unable to repeat the prayer. This was not a simple case of occult subjection but rather one of demonization or obsession.

In cases of obsession and also possession the victim can easily fall into a trance when it comes to renouncing the devil. At other times a person may cry out, "I can't use his name (Jesus), I can't force myself to say it."

What do we do in circumstances like this? One can either command the evil powers in the name of Jesus, or else call some other Christian brothers to join in praying for the subjected person.

In the King James Version of the Bible one finds a very fitting expression for this prayer of renunciation in 2 Corinthians 4:2. There Paul writes: "We have renounced the hidden things."

This renunciation is often followed by a remarkable change. While writing this book a letter reached me containing the following words: "When I wanted to get up, I found I couldn't. It was as if I was bound. Then you came across to me and somehow I managed to get to my feet . . . . In the vestry you asked me a number of questions. You then told me to get down on my knees and to pray a prayer after you. When I did this, I meant it with all my heart. After that I left. It's now ten years since I talked with you. I have never fallen into the same old mistake again. It's gone completely. The day after our conversation I felt quite strange. I was so light and free. It was as if I could fly, as if chains had fallen from me. It was really wonderful."

Not everyone experiences such elated feelings after deliverance, but the change of ownership is still valid no matter how one feels.

The woman whose letter I have just quoted, has continued to grow as a Christian ever since her initial deliverance. She has been able to lead her daughters and her sons-in-law to the Saviour. The whole family has been completely changed. The mother's deliverance and conversion was only the start.

Renunciation is particularly important in cases where natives are converted out of a heathen background. Peter Jamieson, the aborigine chief of the Wongai tribe, in effect confirmed this when he told me, "Many converts backslide through not having renounced before God the various magical practices of their tribe."

6. The forgiveness of sins.

Forgiveness is independent of all human achievement, and neither is it man's by right of confession alone. No, forgiveness is ours solely as a result of the completed work of Christ on the cross. In Ephesians 1:7 Paul declares, "In him we have redemption through his blood, the forgiveness of our trespasses according to the riches of his grace."

The blessing that is ours through confession is grounded upon the promise of 1 John 1:9, "If we confess our sins he is faithful and just and will forgive us our sins and cleanse us from all unrighteousness."

The promise of forgiveness, which is sometimes called absolution, is founded upon the words of Jesus recorded in John 20:23, "If you forgive the sins of any, they are forgiven."

Obviously many complications can arise in this area.

It may be that the minister who tells the confessing person his sins are forgiven, has not been absolved of his own sins by God. If this is the case, is the forgiveness valid? Of course. If God were to wait until he found a minister worthy enough of the task, there would be no forgiveness in the world at all.

But obviously as a rule, the person who absolves another should by the grace of God have been forgiven his own sins.

Another question which arises in people's minds is whether or not an ordained man should always be the one to announce this promise of forgiveness. The answer is, of course not. A Christian doctor, or a Christian road sweeper has more scriptural authority to absolve a person from his sins than an unconverted or unbelieving clergyman.

Now another example which I personally found very moving.

Ex. 76. In 1956 I was speaking in various churches and seminaries in Paris. In the Tabernacle of the Rev. Blocher a student from Haiti came to me to be counselled. He had been ill as a young boy and his parents had taken him on several occasions to some magical healers, the so-called obiahs. Officially his parents had belonged to the Catholic Church, yet whenever the need had arisen, they had immediately sought the sorcerers' advice. In this way the young child's life had been overshadowed by sorcery. He had come to Paris in order to study. Inwardly, however, he had felt ill at ease and had been plagued with depressions. For this reason he had come to see me. He made an open confession of his sins. I then called the minister and another Christian in and together we prayed for the young student. The student then prayed a prayer of renunciation after me. For ten years I never saw him again. One day though at the Berlin Congress an evangelist came up to speak with me. I did not recognize him a first

but then I realized it was the selfsame student I had
counselled ten years previously. By now he had become
a well-known evangelist in his own country. As we talked
together, he told me that he had been completely delivered
after our time together in Paris.

Forgiveness of sins and deliverance from occult oppression completely revolutionize a person's life.

7. Loosing from the powers of darkness.

To loose or to release a person from the devil's grip is
as much a spiritual task as the absolving of a person from
his sins. The principle is based upon the words of Jesus
in Matthew 18:18, "Whatever you loose on earth shall be
loosed in heaven." A merely traditional or liturgical type
of loosing is impossible. Loosing a person is a charismatic
task. In order to accomplish this task one must possess
the gift of discernment together with the spiritual
authority and guidance of the Lord.

Ex. 77. A few years ago I had the opportunity to speak
in six different Bible colleges in England. Among the
students who came to be counselled was a young man
who had already tried to commit suicide on a number of
occasions. This tendency, however, had only appeared
when he started attending the Bible school. It was therefore a fairly good indication that his problem was an
occult one. The attacks of the mentally ill and the manic-
depressives are not triggered off by their religious attitudes
or actions. Occultly subjected people on the other hand
often suffer their first attacks when they seek to follow
Christ or serve him in some way. I advised the young man
to try and find out if anyone in his family had practised
occultism. A single telephone call was sufficient. His
grandmother admitted that the family had indeed practised certain forms of occultism in the past. After confession I loosed the young man in the name of Jesus and
he was delivered.

This loosing, however, must never become something automatic. I personally only exercise this ministry after having first had a very thorough counselling session with the person concerned, and only then if the Lord gives me the inner freedom to do so. On average I think I would only dare 'loose' about 10 to 20 per cent of those I counsel.

Ex. 78. A nurse once came to see me who was being badly plagued by the devil. As a child she had been treated on more than one occasion by an unusually strong sorcerer. Her suffering was enough to move anyone. I felt so concerned for her that I was somewhat prematurely constrained to loose her from her demonic bondage. As a result of this the following night I was attacked quite terribly by the powers of darkness. It taught me a lesson though, not to act too hastily.

There is a possibility that if a person puts too much of his own effort into trying to help the demonically oppressed that a transference will take place.

I am very grateful though for the innumerable examples in front of me illustrating how after confession, renunciation, and loosing in the name of Jesus, people have been able to experience complete liberation and deliverance from the powers of darkness. This is the Lord's doing, and it is marvellous in our eyes.

8. The prayer group.

Counselling the occultly oppressed is really a matter of team-work. The individual counsellor is far too weak to take upon his own shoulders all the problems he meets. The world together with the whole human race is plunging into a night of darkness. The oppression of mankind grows continually greater, while the number of spiritual counsellors able to meet this need ever decreases. Some denominations have only half the number of trained ministers they really need. In addition to this the vast majority of Bible students and students of theology are given no preparation whatever for the ministry of Christian counselling. And the few counsellors that exist in the world are almost crushed under the weight of the inquiries they receive either in person or through the post.

In reality our churches and our Christian fellowships, which should comprise of prayer cells always ready to assimilate and help any who are oppressed by the devil, are not spiritually of age. One could spend a long time lamenting this fact, but we have no desire here to magnify the failings of the twentieth century Church.

In the Scriptures we find the idea of a prayer group expressed in the words of Jesus in Matthew 18:19, "If two or three of you agree on earth about anything they ask, it will be done for them by my Father in heaven." The Early Church gives us an example of how the Christians often used to meet together to pray. In Acts 12:12 we find for example many gathered together for prayer in the house of Mary, the mother of John Mark. Acts 4:31 similarly records a time of prayer after which the whole place was shaken and all those present were filled with the Holy Spirit.

Occultly oppressed people are still very vulnerable even after their actual deliverance. For this reason a small group of Christians should take it upon themselves to continue to care and to pray for them even after their conversion. If necessary the group need only consist of two Christians. They should meet together at least twice or three times a week for perhaps a quarter of an hour at a time in order to pray for the oppressed person. The best thing is for the subjected person to be present as well, yet this is not absolutely necessary. Neither is it essential for the oppressed person to have made an open confession before all the members of the group. This need only have been made before the counsellor at the very start. An example.

Ex. 79. In Cordoba, Argentina, a sick woman visited a spiritist and was subsequently healed. The spiritist had had such strong mediumistic powers that the woman later found that she also possessed the ability to heal. In fact she earned quite a lot of money with this gift. One day she received a visit from Professor Winter, a man I know personally. This Christian doctor knew a great deal about spiritism and spoke to the woman about the damaging effects evil spirits could have on a person's life. The woman was impressed by what the doctor said. On his next visit, beyond all expectation, the woman accepted the Lord Jesus as her own Saviour. The evil spirits immediately started to take their revenge. The woman even saw frogs jumping out of her own mouth — exactly as in the case of Gottliebin Dittus in Germany. During the night she found that her bed was shaken about and she was plagued in every conceivable way. Professor Winter, realizing the need she was in, asked a few Christians to form a prayer group with him in order to regularly pray for the afflicted woman. In the end she was delivered. Today she continues to live a life of sacrifice to her Lord and she gives much to the furtherance of His work. Professor Winter still receives a monthly cheque from her in support of his mission hospital in Argentina.

This example is extremely valuable since it was experienced and recounted to me by a qualified medical doctor. I have in fact twice had the opportunity of speaking at his hospital, the Cruz Blanca Esquil Hospital in Argentina. Without the support of the group of praying Christians, the battle for this bound and oppressed woman would almost certainly have been without success.

9. Prayer and fasting.

Jesus met his disciples one day when they were disillusioned by the fact that they had been unable to heal a possessed boy. "Why could we not cast it out?" they asked the Lord. "Because of your little faith," Jesus replied. "This kind never comes out except by prayer and fasting" (Matt. 17:14—21).

Fasting was a recognized practice in both the Old and the New Testaments. We know that Daniel fasted and prayed for three weeks on one occasion (Dan. 9:3; 10:3), and Jesus himself went without food for forty days in the wilderness.

Over the last few centuries the Catholic Church has turned fasting into a kind of penance. In the Protestant churches on the other hand fasting is almost unheard of today. Yet fasting has still a very meaningful place in the supporting of a person's fervent prayers.

Ex. 80. A Lutheran minister once had a woman come to him one day who for years had been diagnosed by the psychiatrists as suffering from schizophrenia. Since the woman said that in the evenings she saw terrifying faces at her window, and that she was plagued by the thought of committing suicide, the minister realized he might be dealing with a case of occult subjection. He had read my book 'Christian Counselling and Occultism' which in fact says among other things that as spiritists advance in years, they often start seeing faces of the nature the woman had described. He subsequently questioned the woman very thoroughly and then formed a prayer group which determined to pray for her until they saw some signs of improvement in her condition. The Lord blessed their love for the woman by completely healing her.

For some years now during each mission I take, I set aside a special day for prayer and fasting. Invariably some of the Christians in the neighbourhood join me. For example at the Methodist church in Chur, Switzerland, 54 Christians from both the Methodist church and the other churches in the area took part.

In the Rhineland I had the great joy of learning that

following a mission the local minister decided to continue these days of prayer and fasting every month with other Christians from his church. They have now continued this much blessed practice for a number of years with about 20 to 30 people usually taking part. Occasionally the group welcomes one or two occultly oppressed people into its midst, and they continue to pray for them until the Lord hears and answers their cry.

10. The protection of the blood of Christ.

Nothing fills the demons with more fear than the name and the blood of Jesus. If a person dealing with demonically oppressed people fails to use the protection that God has provided for him, he will achieve nothing.

Ex. 81. A missionary in the Far East had a great deal to do with possessed people. Without realizing it, he gradually became influenced himself, and a shadow came to rest on his spiritual life. As time went on he found that all desire to read the Bible had left him and he could not pray. While in this state he returned to Germany. His relatives, noticing the change in him, thereupon formed a prayer group which was strengthened by the presence of another Christian worker. After some weeks the missionary was liberated.

Ex. 82. In no other land has the danger threatening missionaries been shown to me more clearly than in Japan. Although I have now visited as many as 120 different countries, Japan still seems to me to be the hardest mission field to work in. I have had up to 25 different missionaries come to me there for counselling who had become involved in things which would never have been possible for them at home.

If a person has to work in a demonized neighbourhood, he needs the faithful prayer support of his fellow believers as well as the protection of Christ. I would ask my readers at this point to pray for me if they would, for I greatly appreciate the prayer backing of fellow believers. As a result of my work among the occultly oppressed and the possessed I am sometimes stretched to the very limits of my physical, mental and spiritual powers. If it were not for the fact that the Lord had held his hand over me in the past, I would have been ruined long ago.

But our position is not lost. We have a strong tower and mighty fortress in which to take our stand. In Zechariah 2:5 the Lord declares, "I will be to her a wall of fire round about, and will be the glory within her."

The victorious Church, which is one day to be taken up into glory, has this testimony borne to it in Revelation 12:11, "They have overcome Satan by the blood of the Lamb and by the word of their testimony."

> Our hope is built on nothing less
> Than Jesus' blood and righteousness.
> When all around our souls give way,
> He then is all our hope and stay.

Although I have probably mentioned Luther's dream already in one of my books, it is worth repeating here again. In the dream Luther found himself being attacked by Satan. The devil unrolled a long scroll containing a list of Luther's sins and held it before him. On reaching the end of the scroll Luther asked the devil, "Is that all?" "No," came the angry reply, and a second scroll was thrust in front of him. Then, after the second came a third. But now the devil had no more. "You've forgotten something," Luther exclaimed triumphantly. "Quickly, write on each of them, 'The blood of Jesus Christ God's Son cleanses us from all sins!'" The devil let out an awful cry, cursed and disappeared. The blood of Jesus had brought his plans to nought.

"The blood shall be a sign for you," was the message given to the children of Israel in Egypt (Exod. 12:13). The blood was the sign for the Lord to pass over their houses and protect them from the destroying angel. Today the blood of Christ is the sign to us that we too will be spared from the enemy when he attempts to afflict and attack our souls.

The blood of Jesus is our standard.

11. Commanding in the name of Jesus.

There are situations when one can get no further by praying for a person who is demonically oppressed. While Paul and Silas were preaching the gospel at Philippi in Macedonia, a young slave girl with the spirit of divination started following Paul and plaguing him with her cries. After some days Paul could bear it no longer, so turning to the girl he said, "I charge you in the name of Jesus Christ to come out of her." And the spirit came out of her that very hour (Acts 16:18).

When Paul came face to face with the magician Elymas in Cyprus, the same situation arose. Elymas withstood Paul and Barnabas' message. Paul, however, receiving the inner freedom from the Lord and filled with the Holy Spirit said to him, "You son of the devil, you enemy of righteousness, full of all deceit and villainy. Behold, the hand of the Lord is upon you and you shall be blind and unable to see the sun for a time." The battle was hard but the victory was his, for the Lord stood with him.

Ex. 83. Peter Octavian, the Indonesian evangelist, was once faced with a woman magician who started disturbing a meeting he was holding on an island in Indonesia. Fixing his eyes on her he said, "In the name of Jesus I command you to be quiet. Come down to the front row and listen carefully to the gospel." At once the woman stopped talking, and she came to the front and listened for the rest of the meeting.

As we emphasized with loosing, commanding in the name of Jesus is similarly a charismatic act. It can never become a mere formality.

Ex. 84. A young Greek wanted to get closer to God. He went to speak with a priest of the Orthodox Church to ask his advice. The priest was a spiritist and invited the student to come to one of the spiritistic meetings being held in Thessaloniki. Afterwards, however, the student lost any sense of peace he had had, and he started suffering from depressions. It was at this time that he attended a meeting of a Protestant evangelist. There for the first time in his life he heard the gospel concerning Jesus being preached. The message spoke to his heart. Later, in spite of belonging to the Orthodox Church, he went to speak with the evangelist. He started making a confession of his sins, but suddenly he faltered and could not utter another word. "Are you trying to confess something further?" his counsellor asked. The student nodded. The evangelist therefore commanded the powers which were present in the name of Jesus to leave the young man in peace. The confession then continued and the man was able to bring into the light the whole spiritistic story. Through the work of Christ the young student experienced a complete deliverance. He was filled with joy. However, as a result of his over-confidence he suffered a reversal of his condition. That same evening when he had got back to his room, he boasted to Satan, "You can't touch me. I'm able to stand up to you now." At once he suddenly received a terrible blow and fell to the ground paralysed. The next day when he failed to appear at the meal table, someone went to his room and found him still paralysed. The evangelist when he came recognized at once that the devil was at work again, and so he commanded him a second time in the name of Jesus. The Lord was again gracious and the student was delivered. He confessed his rashness and learnt thereby to be much more careful.

In the name of Jesus we have a weapon which is greatly feared by the archenemy of our souls. But we can only wield this weapon if our hands have been cleansed by the blood of Christ.

12. The means of grace.

Almost the world over the appearance of the Church of Christ is that of a spiritually undernourished assembly of Christians. There is so little power within the Church and so little victorious living among the individual members. In saying this, I feel that I am included myself. But what is the reason for our failure?

It is simply that we are not living from the Lord's fullness. The early Christians were able to say, "And from his fullness have we all received, grace upon grace" (John 1:16). The writer of Psalm 87 also knew the secret of this fullness when he wrote, "All my springs are in you."

Everyone who thirsts and seeks satisfaction must come to this source. All who hunger and wish to be nourished must gain access to His storehouses. All who desire the spirit of life must come to Him daily and eat the bread of life. All who desire to build up their faith must make use of the spiritual bricks He has provided. In Acts 2:42 we find them listed: the apostels' teaching, fellowship, the breaking of bread, and prayer.

Ex. 85. One of the most wonderful experiences of my life was to be allowed to visit the 'Jesus family' in the revival area of Indonesia. The majority of my experiences while out there are described in another of my books 'Revival in Indonesia'. Among these Christians I was able to witness events almost identical to those recorded in the Acts of the Apostles. At sunrise neighbouring families meet together to sing and pray, and the sound of their voices is truly marvellous. The literate and the illiterate listen together as the Word of God is read to them. Morning and evening they meet in this way for fellowship, and they break bread together regularly.

Often, however, there is no wine on the island with which to remember the Lord's death. As a result of this the Lord has sometimes actually changed water into wine for them — a thing which for the Western mind will be completely unimaginable. But the selfsame Jesus is in their midst whose voice once cried, "All things are possible to him who believes." Their prayer fellowship is also a thing unknown in the West. The only place I have ever come across something on the same level was in the Korean revival. It was just as if the heavens were opened when they prayed. One could understand maybe for the first time the true significance of the fact that Jesus has opened the doors of Paradise for us to enter again.

If we but had these 'Jesus families' in the West, then those who had been recently liberated from the powers of darkness could be placed within them for protection, for the spiritual atmosphere of such fellowships is a source of tremendous protective power.

When a person is delivered and liberated from his occult oppression, he must really lay hold of the four spiritual elements which go to make up our Christian discipleship. These are again: the Word of God, fellowship with the children of God, the breaking of bread, and continuous prayer.

Yet in spite of everything we need not look with envy or be discouraged by the revival presently taking place in Indonesia. Jesus is the same whether in the revival area or with us. His power is likewise sufficient for us, no matter where we are. This is illustrated in the following example from the West.

Ex. 86. A young girl I know very well, was quite ill for a number of years. She went from one doctor to another. No one could help her. Her family then heard of the spirit healer and miracle doctor called Gröning. Her father took her along to see the man, hoping that he had finally found someone who could heal his daughter.

As they sat in the waiting room, the girl, who had recently accepted the Lord Jesus as her Saviour, felt an evil atmosphere around her. She therefore started to pray. Bruno Gröning now entered the room. He stood in front of the girl and asked her, "Do you believe I can make you better?" "If God gives you the power to heal me, then yes," the girl replied. Gröning's next remark was significant. "There's a force within you that is resisting my healing powers," he said. — This is yet another illustration of the fact that spiritistic and spirit healers reach an impasse when someone prays. Gröning now proceeded to give the patients who had come to see him either balls or sheets of tin foil. This he told them to carry with them throughout the day and to lay it under their pillows at night. They could also take pictures of him if they wanted to in order to lay their hands on them. Immediately after this the girl became very restive. In the end she finally burnt all that Gröning had given her in spite of the fact that it was against her father's wishes. But she felt a little better after this. It was then that she came into contact with a missionary group of Christians who took her under their wing. She confessed everything that God had put on her conscience including her meeting with Gröning. She next prayed a prayer of renunciation after the person who was counselling her. Her counsellor then loosed her from the power of the devil. She now found that she had been delivered from the pressure that had been resting on her and from the fears that had gripped her. This missionary group had become a 'Jesus family' to the young girl.

13. The return of evil spirits.

What we have to say in this section is extremely important and it should drive every true counsellor to a state of personal repentance.

Jesus himself was well aware of the fact that evil

spirits can return to a man after being driven out. In Luke 11 we find him saying, "When the unclean spirit has gone out of a man, he passes through waterless places seeking rest; and finding none he says, 'I will return to my house from which I came.' And when he comes he finds it swept and put in order. Then he goes and brings seven other spirits more evil than himself, and they enter and dwell there; and the last state of that man becomes worse than the first."

I know of a number of terrible instances of this from my own counselling work. Yet before I go on to speak about this subject in more detail, let me first of all try to clear up quite a widespread misunderstanding. I would ask any Christian who engages in this type of counselling work to consider the difference between the following examples.

a) The apparent return of evil spirits.

Ex. 87. An epileptic girl used to attend a Protestant youth group quite regularly. The mother then allowed her daughter to be charmed. As a result of this magical treatment the epilepsy disappeared. However, afterwards both mother and daughter ceased going along to the church. The minister went to see them and inquired why they were staying away from the services. He soon discovered what lay behind their actions and also found out that the 'spirit healer' had given the girl an amulet to wear. Asking them to show him the amulet, he opened it and found inside a piece of paper containing what amounted to be a contract with the devil. It said in effect that in exchange for her healing the devil would be able to have her soul. Both women were terribly frightened by this discovery. They repented immediately and burnt the amulet. Now what happened? The epilepsy returned. But after their confession and repentance the mother and daughter were once again able to pray, and they started to attend the church services once more. But although the illness had returned, it was not a case of the return of evil spirits, but rather just the opposite. The reappearance of the illness was actually an indication that the occult ban had now been broken.

Nevertheless I am not completely happy with the course the story took. Why, I ask, did the minister not pray that the Lord would now heal the girl? We give Jesus a bad name if we act as if the devil can heal but Jesus cannot.

Ex. 88. One of my friends was once more faithful. He had arranged some meetings at which I was to speak. During the mission a young man came to see me to be counselled. As a child he had been charmed and healed by a shepherd. While he was with me he made an open confession of his sins and renounced the contact he had had with occultism. He left the room a delivered and forgiven man. Later when the mission had ended, I had to leave the area. In the meantime, however, the young man started to suffer from the same disease he had been afflicted with as a child. His mother became very angry and visited my friend complaining bitterly about the counsel I had given her son, since in her mind the only result had been that his former illness had returned. But my friend's faith was sufficient for the situation and he replied to the mother, "What the devil can do, the Lord Jesus can do a thousand times better. We must therefore ask the Lord to come and heal your son." They prayed together with the result that the young man was healed.

It is really a gift of God to be given a friend like this to accompany one in the spiritual march of life. There have been other people who have arranged meetings whose attitude, instead of being spiritual, has rather been critical, so much so that sometimes they have said, "That's what you get when you ask men like this to speak. They only disturb the peace of the church and confuse the people."

This has even been my own experience sometimes. It is not everyone who can scale the heights of the Christian faith. In the battle against the powers of darkness one meets many Christian workers who are both inexperienced and lacking in authority. Although I am only too well aware of the misery and poverty of my own heart, our real comfort is in this, that we have a Lord who is ever at hand to help the needy. And it is among such people that I belong.

People have sometimes criticised me for having occasionally quoted from the apocrypha, but in spite of the fact that it obviously cannot be placed on the same footing as the Old and New Testaments, one is nevertheless still able to find wonderful pearls within its pages.

The hope of the poor

"The prayer of the humble pierces the clouds,
he will not be consoled until it reaches the Lord,
he will not desist until the Most High visits him."
                                                    Sirach 35:17.
"The Lord delivers the needy when he calls,
the poor and him who has no helper."   Psalm 72:12.
"Thou, O Lord, art a stronghold to the poor,
a stronghold to the needy in his distress."   Isaiah 25:4.
"The needy shall not be forgotten, and the hope
of the poor shall not perish for ever."   Psalm 9:18.

b) The actual return of evil spirits.

Experiences involving the actual return of evil spirits illustrate our utter helplessness in these circumstances. If anyone has ever engaged in the struggle for the soul of an oppressed person, he will have been made to realize his own insufficiency to meet the need, but at the same time will have become conscious of the power that issues from our Lord and Saviour Jesus Christ.

Ex. 89. During the second world war a woman became friendly with an army officer. In the course of their friendship they both subscribed themselves to the devil with their own blood. After the military collapse of Germany the officer committed suicide. Later he appeared to the woman and told her that she too should take her own life. However, she refused to do this and was driven to seek the help of some Christians she knew. The Christians prayed for her a great deal and in the end the woman repented and decided to follow Christ. From this moment on though, the attacks of darkness became even worse. She was tortured day and night. She then came into contact with a counsellor who had had some experience in dealing with the demonically oppressed. Together with him she prayed a prayer of renunciation and he loosed her in the name of Jesus from the forces which were continually tormenting her. All seemed to go well for a while. For a number of months she remained free of conflict and was able to pray and hold to her faith. However, all of a sudden the attacks reappeared. She went back to see the counsellor. At once he called some other Christians together so that they might regularly pray for her. The battle is not yet over. When the powers of darkness return, the battle is always fiercer than before.

Very often one finds that the powers of darkness return when a person is liberated in a Christian atmosphere and then has to return and live in an atmosphere of occultism and sorcery. This is frequently what happens in the case of young people from spiritistic families, who are converted when away from home and later have to return and live in the demonically effected house of their parents. The following example of this comes from Holland.

Ex. 90. A teenage boy came from a home in which sorcery is still practised. On beginning work in a new

Christian environment he started suffering from such strange disturbances that the local doctor was convinced he must have developed a tumor of some sort. However, when the boy was counselled the strange symptoms disappeared and he was completely delivered. This is a good indication that he had been suffering rather from a demonic form of oppression inherited from his parents than from a tumor. During his holidays though, he returned to stay with his parents for a few months. This resulted in his old oppression making an appearance again. The battle had to be fought all over again.

People who have been delivered from occult oppression and yet have to return again and live in an occult or spiritistic atmosphere never find real and lasting peace. I usually find that I have to advise young people stemming from such environments, "Stay away from your parents — or from your uncle, aunt or relation — if they are not prepared to forsake their occult practices and interests." This advice is not always appreciated however. In fact, on occasions I have been actually rebuked for having given a person advice of this nature.

Finally, repeating what we have just been saying, anyone who fails to act on all that the Bible says for our protection will live in continuous danger of falling victim once more to the influence of the exorcised spirits.

14. The weapons of this warfare.

There are battles even now taking place in the unseen world, the existence and the severity of which we have absolutely no idea. Occasionally the Bible gives us a glimpse of this situation.

In Jude 9 for example, we have a short account of the battle between the archangel Michael and the devil concerning the body of Moses. In Daniel 10:13 we hear too of the struggle between Michael and the angel prince of Persia; a story which seems to indicate that angels of protection exist not only for people, but possibly also for whole nations.

Turning next to Matthew 4 we read of the conflict between Jesus and Satan, a conflict which spanned the whole world and was watched by angels who ministered to Jesus when the devil left him.

Occasionally these heavenly battles become visible to the eyes of God's people here below. One need only think of the story of Elisha's servant who, on seeing the Syrian army surrounding the city, cried out in fear, "Alas, my master. What shall we do?" Then Elisha spoke those now unforgettable words, "Fear not, for those who are with us are more than those who are with them" (2 Kings 6:15). Next Elisha prayed that the Lord would open the eyes of his young servant, and suddenly the servant saw that the mountains around them were full of the horses and chariots of the Lord.

Today these battles are raging more than ever before. The final conflict has already begun. The heavens are ringing with the war cries of evil spirits. Yet all is not lost. We are not alone. There is Someone with us who is greater than all those that are against us.

Ex. 91. Peter Octavian recounted to me a confrontation the Christians had had with the Moslems in Indonesia. The Christians had arranged an open air meeting when suddenly a large crowd of angry Moslems rounded the corner intent on breaking up the meeting. Peter turned to those with him and said, "Have no fear, those who are with us are more than those who are with them." Then, just as the crowd of Moslems was drawing near, unexpected help suddenly came from the audience which had already gathered to hear the Christians' message. A senior officer of the Indonesian army suddenly stood up and spoke to the approaching crowd. "I have come here to listen to what these people have to say," he shouted. "If you cause any disturbance I will call the army to deal

with you. Either go away, or sit down and listen." With
that the whole crowd became quiet and sat down. Jehovah-
jireh — the Lord will provide.

Ex. 92. The devil unsuccessfully attempted to disrupt
a meeting I was speaking at in Curitiba, Brazil. There
were three women in the church, all suffering from
various forms of occult subjection. One of the women
in spite of her oppression had been a member of a Christian group for 30 years. Now at the meeting she continually felt constrained to shout out, "It's all lies, it's all
lies." The second women was the daughter of an active
charmer and during my talk she suddenly fell into a
trance. The third woman at the same time heard a voice
inside her saying, "Blaspheme against God and start
cursing him." However, none of them in fact accomplished
what the devil had commanded them to do. I was able to
finish speaking without disturbance. After the meeting
the first woman had come to us and confessed what
had been going on. Without our knowledge the Lord
himself had met and defeated the secret attack of the
unseen world.

When engaged in these battles we need more than
anything else the armour of God, without which we
cannot hope to stand. In Ephesians 6:14—16 Paul men-
tions the shield of faith, the helmet of salvation and the
sword of the Spirit. If we lack these, we will fall easy
prey to the enemy.

How then can we carry the shield of faith? In my
personal prayers I adopt the following basic principle:
it is better to exercise faith from the very start and be
prepared to let God disappoint you — although if you
do so this will not happen — than to fail to exercise faith
and thereby disappoint God from the very outset.

How can we use the helmet of salvation to protect
ourselves? Satan flees when he sees us standing at the
foot of the cross. The person who leaves the place of the

cross, however, will surely fall victim to the enemy who lies in wait for all those who leave the victorious ground of their salvation.

Finally, how can we make use of the sword of the Spirit? When I read the Bible I make a habit of underlining certain verses which I then repeat to myself over and over again during the day in order to learn them off by heart. Of Mary the mother of Jesus it is written, "And she pondered these things in her heart." The words that we continually turn over in our minds and consider in our hearts are ever renewed by the Holy Spirit and they become to us a source of great strength. Luther is once recorded as having said the daring words, "One must rub the promises of God into His ears until He hears our cry."

If a person is loosed from his occult oppression, he must be very careful to make use of every means of help recommended to him in the pages of the Scriptures.

Ex. 93. When the Spaniards under Ferdinand Cortez attacked the Aztecs in 1519, they almost despaired at first when their arrows started to bounce off the breastplates of the Spanish soldiers. After a while, however, they discovered that the legs of their attackers were unprotected. Immediately they started to aim lower and succeeded in inflicting serious losses on the Spanish.

The devil too, soon becomes aware of our most vulnerable points. We must therefore be ever on guard against those fiery darts that strike low and wound us below our armour. He will always attack us at our weakest point, be it our pride, our money, impurity, laziness, anger, or whatever it may be. The victory will not come easily. In God's kingdom we have to fight. But the battle is not fought in our own strength, but rather in the strength of Him to whom all power in heaven and upon earth has been given.

15. Realizing the victory.

Christians in America have a hymn whose refrain reads:

> Realize the victory,
> Realize the victory.

Although I can remember the tune, the actual words of the hymn escape me at the moment. Perhaps an American reader would be willing to send me the words of the whole hymn.

The Bible's theme is not one of weary resignation but rather of triumph and victory. In 1 Corinthians 15:57 Paul rejoices with the words, "Thanks be to God who gives us the victory through our Lord Jesus Christ." In the same way the apostle John writing to Christians affirms, "Little children, you are of God and *have* overcome them."

> The victory is complete,
> an accomplished fact.

Christ *has* disarmed the principalities and powers and triumphed over them in his cross (Col. 2:15). This victory is the foundation of our triumph today. No matter how difficult or how wearing the counselling of occultly subjected or even possessed people may be, the fact remains that the victory is ours through what Christ has done.

Let us turn to a scriptural example. In Exodus 14 we have the wonderful story of the deliverance of the children of Israel as they were just about to be overtaken by the army of Pharaoh. The people in fear began to reproach Moses and accuse God. In front of them lay the sea and behind them the chariots of the enemy. There was no escape. Moses did the only thing possible and turned to God in prayer. But he must have not only prayed, he must have cried aloud to God, so great was the need and so great the urgency. And then the Lord replied, "Moses, why do you cry to me? Tell the people of Israel to go forward" (verse 15).

Victory was already theirs, although they knew nothing of it. Oh, how often I have heard the Lord say to me in times of conflict,

"Why do you cry to me? Go forward. Act!"

This is all the Lord requires of us. We must step forward in faith and act. But when must we do this?

In hopeless situations!

I have often found myself in circumstances which have seemed more than hopeless. There was no way out, no light to show me the way, no help at hand. "Why do you cry out as if God did not exist, as if no salvation were prepared?" Oh that we would realize the victory and thereby bring honour to our Lord.

Ex. 94. I have altogether on six occasions visited the continent of Africa. Many is the time I have heard talk of the sharp conflict that exists there between the Christian message and the undiluted heathenism in the land. In the Congo a missionary was plagued for years by the local chief witch-doctor. This was the subject of much prayer on the mission field. Gradually, however, the situation came to a head. One Sunday the missionary called the Christians together for a special time of prayer. The witch-doctor had threatened to inflict a terrible blow on the Christians that day. He had assembled his followers together on a nearby hill. A heavy thunderstorm started to approach. Then, as it passed over, a single flash of lightning was seen to strike. Shortly afterwards a messenger arrived at the church. The witch-doctor had been struck by the lightning and killed.

Salvation was at hand. The missionary church had been allowed to enter into it.

Ex. 95. A young man came to me for counselling. As a boy he had been charmed against an illness. As I prayed with him, he began to curse and blaspheme. I realized that prayer would achieve nothing. In my heart I turned to the Lord for strength and commanded, "In the name of Jesus I command you to be quiet." Immediately he quietened down and began to praise and glorify the Lord of his own accord. The change was amazing. It was the Lord's doing.

16. Complete surrender.

While I was dealing with the worst case of possession I have ever met, I asked the voices coming from the possessed person, "Why don't you leave him alone?" The demons replied in English, "We have possessed him because he didn't surrender his life completely to the Lord."

What a serious warning this should be to all believers. The powers of darkness will seize the slightest opportunity to try and gain entrance into our lives.

When a person is delivered from a state of occult subjection, he must withhold nothing in his life from the Lord. Those areas which are not surrendered to his Lord will soon be occupied again by the enemy.

There is a great difference between saying that we are prepared to live our lives according to the dictates of the Lord Jesus, and saying that the Lord can rule our lives for us. This is what He waits for — the command to take over. If we hope to stand in the battle, Jesus must become the Lord of our time, the Lord of our strength, the Lord of our wills, the Lord of our possessions, the Lord of our plans, and the Lord of our decisions.

Jesus said in Matthew 11:27, "All things have been delivered to me by my Father." We must ask ourselves, does this include us?

Only when Jesus is our Lord will he protect us from the lordship of others.

Ex. 96. An experience of one of my friends illustrates this quite wonderfully. For years this person had been engaged in work among the occultly oppressed, and in his preaching he used to warn people strongly of the dangers involved in occultism. One day a doctor phoned him and said to him, "I have books on magic which I actually use in my work. It made me angry therefore to hear you say these things are dangerous. Because of this I tried to use my magical powers against you but they didn't work. I find that there's a power around you and protecting you which is greater than mine. I must carry the consequences of this now myself." The consequences were dreadful. Instead of turning to Christ for help, the doctor committed suicide the next day.

Besides this magician's terrible end, there is something else that should be mentioned. My friend had felt nothing of the magical attacks being made on him. The Stronger One with him had held His hand of protection over him. This is a message of great comfort to all those who have to engage in the battles and the difficulties of the Christian life.

"He who is with us is greater than he who is in the world," and, "If God be for us who can be against us?" (1 John 4:4; Rom. 8:31).

The atmosphere of the Bible.

The sixteen steps we have just considered bring us to an end of our consideration of the problem of counselling the occultly oppressed. One must never imagine, however, that we have somehow arrived at a set method of dealing with such people. What we have been saying is not a recipe. The Lord in his sovereignty can at any time bypass each and every one of these steps as we saw in Ex. 62. We have merely been considering these things to ensure that we are fully equipped for the conflict, for these weapons of counselling have proved effective now over a number of years. But now we must touch upon another important factor of this work.

Stories of possession exist among all the world's religions, be it Animism, Islam, Buddhism, Judaism, or Christianity. The methods by which the demons are exorcised are likewise as varied. Yet true deliverance is only possible through Christ. Only the Lord has the authority to deliver a person from Satan's power.

"Know that the Son of man has authority on earth" (Mark 2:10).

It is also very important to remember when counselling and caring for the occultly oppressed that this kind of counsel will only thrive in the right spiritual atmosphere. One must never look upon a person and his needs as just another 'case', or as some new 'sensation', or 'object of investigation'. True deliverance will never be forthcoming in an unscriptural atmosphere — even if the battle for the oppressed person appears to be very dramatic. We must be on our guard against every kind of excess, and above all against exhibitionism. Let us therefore be:

> Sound in our faith,
> Sober in our thoughts,
> Honest and scriptural in our attitude.

III. *All Things are Delivered unto Him.*

We come now to one final and crucial point. We find ourselves today in a time of great chaos and confusion. Only when the Antichrist appears will the situation become worse. Let us then just spotlight the present state of affairs.

In the studio of the largest broadcasting station in New York I spoke on the Long John Nebel Show together with a passionate believer of world Utopianism. He opposed my belief that the world was out of joint. He argued, "Life is so wonderful. The world is such a lovely place to live in. The only people who paint a black picture are the prophets of doom." The very same day that he said this, a gang of narcotic smugglers was arrested with 6 pounds of the drug LSD in their possession. The market price at the time of this amount of LSD was about £60,000,000. It would have been sufficient to send about 30 million Americans into a nightmarish land of dreams for several hours.

Behold, the world of today!

In May 1969 I was sitting in a meeting with about 50 young people. Over the building in which we were met, the red flag was flying, while pictures of Lenin and communist slogans decorated the walls of the room we were in. The place was known to the local inhabitants as 'the red tower'. A heated argument was developing. The young people had the impression they were always right. Then came the turning point of the discussion. A young girl who had just sat her final examination in theology and who was a regular member of the group stood up and shouted out, "Jesus was really a homosexual." I jumped to my feet. "That's blasphemy," I cried. "I can't stay here any longer. I'm going." But even as I left the room, another student called out after me, "And Mary was a prostitute."

Behold, the theology of today!

And now a third illustration of the present world scene. It comes from North Korea. Already for many years Christians have been fleeing from the north to the south of Korea. Yet not all have managed to escape, and many martyrs have been claimed by the communist regime of the North. I will quote one of the ugliest acts of perse- cution in order to try and move the Christians of the West to pray more earnestly for their brothers behind the Iron Curtain. Some 10-year-old children were discov- ered meeting together in a secret Sunday school. The communist torturers prepared a terrible end for the class. Thrusting chopsticks down the children's ears they destroyed their eardrums and thereby made it impossible for them ever to hear the gospel message of salvation again.

Behold, the politics of today!

Our story now turns to a senior government official. His name was Pilate. It was a matter of remaining on good terms with the influential leaders of the Jewish nation. Against his own will and against his own conscience he delivered up the One despised of men. The prisoner was beaten, a crown of thorns was thrust down on his head, and he was arrayed in a purple robe. The proud yet cowardly Roman then brought him out to the crowd. Prophetically he said the unforgettable words:

Behold, the man!

In this decaying world with its satanically inspired theology and its demonic politics there stands a Man whose back bends under the weight of every burden, sorrow and trial. A Man apart and different from all other men.

Did his life just end in obscurity? Did his ideals merely end in death? Were his dreams just a hopeless fantasy which followed him to the grave?

No, He is a Man beyond compare. In the form of the lowest He was the Highest. Though clothed in weakness He carried within Himself the power of the Strongest. He is the Man who as Son of God became man, leaving heaven to open heaven to mankind — and behold, He is coming soon.

He will come to destroy and to renew. He will come to abolish the satanic theology of the false prophet of the pit. He will come to smite the political beast. He will come to end the inwardly corrupt civilization of the West and renew the world in righteousness. He must reign and He must act, for God has put all things in subjection under His feet. Above and beyond the catastrophy awaiting this world He stands, and His promise is with Him:

"Surely I am coming soon,"
"Behold, I make all things new."

PART TWO

Dr. Alfred Lechler

A. THE NEED TO DISTINGUISH BETWEEN DISEASE AND THE DEMONIC

Most, if not all of us, have at some time or other in our lives come into contact with people exhibiting abnormal mental characteristics, whose whole behaviour pattern has been of a rather repellent nature. On such occasions we often find it extremely difficult to know how we ought to react, and for this reason we usually endeavour to discover the underlying cause of the problem in order to avoid offending or harming the person by some incorrect attitude or action on our part. Although the conclusion one usually reaches is that the disturbance is basically pathological in nature, it is nevertheless quite legitimate to ask in many cases whether or not the demonic is involved. In fact this question, disease or the demonic, is not only of importance from the medical point of view, but also from the point of view of Christian counselling and from the purely human standpoint.

Distinguishing between demonic oppression and mental illness is, however, fraught with many difficulties. On the one hand many people closely involved in work among the mentally ill refuse point-blank to accept the possibility of any form of demonic influence whatever, claiming that the whole problem can be explained quite adequately by reference to either depth-psychology or psychopathology. Yet on the other hand, many Christian workers are inclined to the view that the demonic is lurking behind all abnormal phenomena connected with

the emotional and spiritual life of a person. We must
therefore endeavour to distinguish as clearly as we
possibly can between disease and the demonic.

I believe that the Christian psychiatrist has a very
important contribution to make with regard to this task.
However, he finds himself in a rather difficult position.
For example, he cannot simply deny the existence of the
demonic, although present day psychiatric theory and
modern theology both adopt this attitude. In fact in
certain circles anyone who even dares to mention the
word 'demon' is immediately classified as being slightly
abnormal. But it is equally true to say that the Christian
psychiatrist also finds it impossible to accept the view,
which is quite widespread among some believers, that
there is a very close connection between all forms of
mental illness and the demonic. His aim therefore must
be to investigate all cases of alleged demonic oppression
with complete impartiality.

First of all then, are we justified in talking about the
demonic? Most definitely! People are today recognizing
more and more that the demonic is by no means just
some outdated biblical concept. Indeed, demonology has
played no small part in the history of the Church from
the time of Christ right on through to the present day.
The Catholic Church in this respect still reveals a remarkable open-mindedness on the subject of possession, and
is still in retention of special rules and doctrines concerning the question of exorcism.

Although the word 'demonic' is still in fairly common
use today, to the majority of people it merely conveys
a vague notion of strange, unearthly and evil forces.
Those who discern the presence of a real and personal
power behind these forces are generally treated with
derision. Yet on closer investigation it becomes apparent
that this Personality is in fact the very Enemy of God
and a possessor of much power. To those who realize

this, the demonic is no longer just some long discredited concept, but rather a terrible reality with which one must ever increasingly reckon today. Is it not true to say that definite demonic forces were visibly at work in the actions of certain personalities during the Second World War? Is not the present growth in violence, murder, robbery and licentiousness, and the ever increasing hatred and strife to be found in our world, a clear sign of the devil's handiwork? In fact, are not these phenomena but a confirmation of the truth of the teachings of Scripture? How can one accept the present day de-mythologizing of the Bible, when it fails utterly in doing justice to the Scripture's veracity? How can one say that Jesus was merely conforming to an erronious Jewish belief when he drove demons out of people? One can be absolutely certain that as the Son of God, Jesus had an accurate understanding of human nature and the human situation. We are therefore more than justified in accepting his statements and his actions at their face value, even when he was dealing with the demonically oppressed.

The Bible itself clearly furnishes us with an answer to our question, disease or the demonic. The distinction can be seen first of all in the attitude Jesus himself adopted to this problem. When He sent the twelve out to preach the kingdom of heaven, he also told them to, "Heal the sick ... and cast out demons" (Matt. 10:1—8). In the same way in Mark 16:17, 18 he gives a list of the signs that would follow those who believe: "In my name they will cast out demons ... they will lay their hands on the sick and they will recover." The fact that Jesus distinguished clearly between disease and possession is also revealed in the way he dealt with the deaf mute in Mark 7, and the deaf and dumb boy in Mark 9. In the first story we read of Jesus putting his fingers into the man's ears and touching his tongue saying, "Be opened," after which the man's ears were opened and his tongue re-

leased, whereas in the second story he drove a demon
out of the young boy with the words, "You deaf and
dumb spirit, I command you, come out of him." Then
again, Jesus sent a message to Herod saying, "Behold,
I cast out demons and perform cures" (Luke 13:32).

In the same way the apostles too distinguished between
illness and demon possession. Mark comments for example
(1:32, 34), "They brought to him all who were sick or
possessed with demons .... And he healed many who
were sick with various diseases, and cast out many demons." And in Mark 6:13 we read, "And they cast out
many demons, and anointed with oil many that were sick
and healed them." (cf. Mark 3:10, 11 and Luke 7:21).
For these reasons we are duty bound, when dealing with
the mentally and emotionally disturbed, to stress the need
to differentiate between disease and the demonic.

B. WHAT IS THE DEMONIC?

We must first of all make it clear what we mean by the
term demonic. The word is used to describe the influence
of Satan and his demons on people, his aim being to lure
such people into sin and to poison their spiritual lives
in order to get them into his power. Satan achieves his
goal through demonic subjection and possession, whereby
his victims are afflicted and troubled in all kinds of ways,
having their emotional and mental lives indelibly stamped
by symptoms which betray his interest in them.

If we turn to the scriptural accounts of either Saul or
Job, we will see that this demonic activity is not only
permitted by God, but sometimes takes place under his
direction. Just as God gives his Holy Spirit to those who
obey him, so too He can send an evil spirit upon a person
who persistently opposes his voice or who falls into
gross sin, and He can allow that spirit to bind the person

and dominate his life. Thus we find God sending an evil spirit to King Saul which tormented him, filling him with unrest, anger, fear and murderous intent (1 Sam. 16:14, 15; 18:10—12). In the case of Job, God gave Satan permission to attack him for a period of time in order to prove his steadfastness and faith (Job 1:12; 2:5, 6). God is sovereign in heaven and on earth, neither Satan nor his demons are outside his control. The powers of darkness can do nothing to hinder the will of God. God has set a limit beyond which they cannot go (Mark 1:27; Job 2:5,6).

In answer to the various people who sometimes ask me what medical experience says concerning the reality of the demonic, I will in the following paragraphs list some of the typical symptoms of demonic subjection and possession. These I hope will introduce us more intimately to the whole problem of the demonic. But before I do let me first of all quote the words of Bieneck: "A person will only recognize the demonic if, as a result of his Christian discipleship and his living relationship with the Bible, he has developed the ability to discern its presence."

I. *Demonic Subjection.*

Demonic subjection is a surprisingly common occurrence. The term itself refers to the condition of a person who is bound and subject to Satan's power. We read for example in John 13:2, "And during supper, when the devil had already put it into the heart of Judas Iscariot to betray him...", and in Luke 13:16, of the woman who had been bound by Satan for eighteen years. In a similar fashion Paul writes in 2 Tim. 2:26 of men who have been ensnared by the devil and captured by him to do his will. It emerges from these passages that Satan has the power to bind people to himself, and to thereby enforce his will upon them and even to afflict them with various diseases while they remain prisoners to him.

Yet the question arises, how can a person fall into Satan's power? Or, putting it in other words, what are the underlying causes of demonic subjection? There are several answers to this question. If a person blatantly lives a life of sin and persistently resists the Spirit of God and remains completely unrepentant, or if a person carries the sin of murder or abortion on his conscience, or has committed purjury or practised incest, if he has cursed his fellow men or blasphemed against the cross or against Christ, the Holy Spirit, or God, then he will have laid himself open to the devil's attacks. Every curse is in fact a cry to the devil, and can for this reason lead a person into bondage. But demonic subjection can also arise in the life of a person cursed by someone already in the devil's power.

Then again, it is particularly easy for those who engage in occult practices to fall victim to demonic subjection. Such practices include visiting a fortune-teller who has occult powers, spiritistic enquiring of the dead, charming, the reading of books on sorcery and horoscopes, super-stitious practices, as for example the wearing of amulets or the use of so-called letters of protection, and even the use of a rod or pendulum if it is allied to clairvoyance. But above all, a conscious subscribing of oneself to the devil, particularly with one's own blood, will result in a terrible form of demonic subjection and oppression. Formal contracts with the devil of this nature take place much more frequently than one would care to think, but fear prevents many people from confessing what they have done. The motive behind this surrendering of one's life and soul to Satan is usually the desire to have some special wish fulfilled.

However, it is not only the active engagement in occult sins like those we have just mentioned which leads to demonic subjection, but one frequently finds that people whose parents or ancestors have practised sorcery also fall under the ban of the devil. In fact, powerful sorcerers and mediums often seek to transfer their occult powers over to some relative or friend, be it an adult or child, before they die. Later the people onto whom the powers have been transferred suddenly become aware of their strange inheritance.

And so, in all these ways either knowingly or unknowingly, man lays claim to the services of the devil. His motive may vary from a desire for something that has previously been denied him, be it wealth or some form of worldly fortune, to a desire to uncover the future which God in his purposes has hidden from him. But whatever it may be, Satan is only too willing to oblige, although in the end the result is always disastrous. One therefore finds that people who are charmed are often healed, and that those who visit fortune-tellers often receive accurate information concerning the future, that is if the fortune-teller in question is really in contact with demonic forces. In the same way devilish contracts are frequently fulfilled and curses against others often succeed — except when uttered against genuine Christians. But the devil does not give his services free of charge. If a person turns to him for help, he binds him with heavy chains and brings him into subjection. And the person will remain bound, unable in his own strength to break loose. God has forsaken him and has given him up (Rom. 1:24, 26, 28), and more often than not ominous symptoms appear in the person's emotional and mental life, betraying the terrible bondage.

With this we are brought face to face with the question of the actual characteristics of demonic subjection, which I have been forced to witness time and time again in the many years of my psychiatric practice. However, since the devil is able to exercise such a varied influence on people, it is difficult to give an exhaustive or completely reliable description of the characteristics signs of his bondage. In spite of this though, in many cases of demonic oppression the outline is clear enough, the symptoms more often than not making their appearance in the psychical life of the person concerned.

One of the first things to become subject to the devil's influence is a person's thoughts and feelings. This often results in a complete attitude of indifference to any spiritual influence, and to an open rejection of any belief in God. The Word of God loses its power to speak, and God's promises become meaningless. The person finds he can only entertain evil thoughts in his mind and ideas which are opposed to God. He is gripped with a passion for lying and impure thoughts. Indeed, the desire to lie so fills him that he does so unconsciously. In spite of feeling no remorse for his sins, he will be plagued with a continous feeling of restlessness, with a lack of peace, and depressive moods. The mere sight of a crucifix or a picture of Jesus disturbs him. A terrible fear frequently haunts him, arising from the feeling of being persecuted day and night, and he often feels as if someone is standing behind him, or is standing beside his bed at night.

Yet Satan not only seeks to govern a person's thoughts and feelings through demonic subjection, but also a person's will. For this reason the oppressed person will refuse to obey God, and will sin quite openly, knowing full well that his actions are wrong. Inwardly he feels a compulsion to do those things demanded of him by the devil. He is thus liable to suddenly rebel against God or blaspheme, to have fits of fury and be defiant towards other people, exhibiting spite, enmity, excitability and violent behaviour. When angry, he curses himself and will curse and hate others who have offended him. Reconciliation is a thing unknown to him. Sometimes on account of some slight disagreement, or often for no real reason at all, he hits out at or curses his own relatives and friends, and even expresses a desire to kill them. He may be completely overcome by an excessive sexual craving, or by a passion for abnormal sexual activities, or by a craving for alcohol, nicotine or drugs, and so on. An irresistable urge to injure himself can also take possession of him, and he may frequently attempt to put his thoughts of suicide into action. On many occasions he will unconsciously do things to spite God. This may include destroying his Bible or tearing the pages out which he feels accuse him, burning religious literature, throwing his hymn book across the room, or tearing down religious texts. If he is given a Christian magazine, he may utter some rude remark or blaspheme, and without looking at it tear it up and throw it away, or tread it under foot. On top of all this he will frequently call on the devil to help him, although he will endeavour to conceal all his evil thoughts and deeds since his master, Satan, the prince of darkness, fights against sin being brought in the light for fear of it being confessed and forgiven.

A very frequent sign of demonic subjection is an inability to repeat aloud or to write the name of Jesus. One often finds that the oppressed person can only do this after an inner battle, and then only with a distorted face or a mechanical voice. Satan has no desire to be reminded of the Name of the One who defeated him on the cross at Golgotha. Thus, when the subjected person is asked to repeat a sentence or a prayer containing the word 'Jesus', he usually remains dumb. Sometimes the mere sound of the word is enough to stir him into a state of inner excitement, or cause him to frown. He can also refuse to sing a hymn which addresses Christ or look at a picture of Jesus, and will put aside any book in which he finds Jesus' name. One such person who wrote to me, desiring to refer to Jesus in his letter, could only do so by writing, "He who hangs on the cross. . . .

you know who I mean." If the oppressed person is invited to pray, then he may either feel as if he is choking, or he will find a series of mocking and blasphemous thoughts arising within his mind. In addition to this he may find it impossible to fold his hands in prayer. Conversely he shies away from all talk about the devil and Satan, and about demons and hell. All forms of spiritual help and counsel make him restless and unfriendly.

One particular guise in which demonic subjection may appear, is in the form of mediumistic abilities. If this is the case, in addition to the symptoms already mentioned, the subjected person may occasionally fall into a state of unconsciousness (self-hypnosis), or exhibit powers of mesmerism, telepathy or clairvoyance, or walk in his sleep, display extraordinary feats of memory, or develop the ability to use a rod or a pendulum. However, it must be stressed that not all of these symptoms in themselves are necessarily a sign of the demonic.

The degree of demonic subjection varies a great deal and depends upon the amount of unforgiven sin which the oppressed person has heaped upon himself. In the case of the less severe forms of the demonic, the oppression may only become apparent after a thorough period of counselling.

If in fact an oppressed person undergoes sustained counselling and is given authoritative spiritual advice, it is quite possible for him to succumb to a typical state of inner confusion and conflict. While he may express a genuine desire to become a Christian and to follow Christ, he will be unable to do so since an inner voice will prevent him. "I would like to become a Christian, but I can't. There's a barrier between myself and Jesus," were the actual words of a person I once counselled. To begin with, even though he wants to, he finds it impossible to accept the fact that God loves him and is willing to forgive him. On numerous occasions one hears these people exclaim, "I'll never be saved. I'll never have any peace. If only I could cry, but my heart feels like stone." When he turns to the Bible or tries to pray, a revulsion comes over him as the enemy of souls seeks to prevent him being influenced by the things of God. And then even if the oppressed person manages to open his Bible or begin to pray, an immense tiredness will overwhelm him, or he will find it impossible to concentrate, or his mind will suddenly become filled with distracting thoughts. Occasionally he may be unable to bend his knees to pray, or if he is praying he will suddenly stand up and exclaim angrily that it is all quite meaningless. This inner conflict and unrest usually is a source of much suffering and distress to him. He can often hear inner voices and suggestions coming into his mind without knowing what they really mean. And if he believes Satan is influencing him, a permanent restlessness will plague him, either on account of his having resisted the enemy's promptings, or as a result of the terrible guilt he feels for having obeyed his will.

The oppressed people who experience this inner turmoil, clearly recognize the enormity of their sins, but they find themselves unable at first to truly repent. They may in fact desire to be delivered from their bondage, and yet time and time again they are compelled to return to their old sinful habits, being incapable of offering any serious resistance. A person like this may one moment find himself attracted towards what is good and determined to hand his life over to God, and the next moment he hates the good, loves evil, doubts God, and distrusts the Bible. For a while he may exhibit a friendly attitude to those around him, then all of a sudden, he will turn round and answer back spitefully or insolently, and may even resort to using insults and filthy language. A friend may on one occasion receive a friendly letter from him and the next moment be handed some scrap of paper full of nothing but reproaches and lies. If he attempts to befriend genuine Christians he feels uncomfortable in their presence and may begin to mock them and refer to them as 'those pious people'. During church services he sometimes finds it almost impossible not to laugh. He turns the pages of his hymn book without thinking, or simply goes to sleep. If the gospel is preached he often becomes very restless or even angry, and the conflict and doubt within him only increases, leaving him in a worse state than before. One day he is moody, unresponsive and stubborn, the next day he starts to call on God for mercy as a feeling of despair and desperation overcomes him. One moment he promises never to drink again, or to break with all his other bad habits, yet in next to no time he has gone back on his word. Thoughts of suicide can suddenly be replaced by a fear of death and final judgement. He will often express the desire not to lie anymore, but finds he just cannot stop himself, and cursing will be another thing from which he cannot free himself. The secret desire to murder someone is a persistent thought in the mind of many, and to this effect a woman once wrote to me and said, "Maybe only when I have committed murder will I be able to listen to God. I don't want to do things wrong, but I'm forced to."

Demonic subjection can in particular be recognized by a person's reaction to the Christian counsellor. While the oppressed person may at times be quite prepared to receive counsel and to confess his sins, he can suddenly exhibit a marked distrust of the counsellor and refuse point-blank to talk any more about his own evil thoughts and actions. He may simply be unable to open his own mouth, or the thing he wished to confess may all of a sudden just disappear from his mind. Then again, if he does manage to confess some of his sins, he will nevertheless purposely conceal others from the counsellor. In fact someone once begged me saying, "Keep on asking me all the time if I'm really telling the truth, and if I've confessed everything." At other times the subjected person will, just before his appointment with the counsellor, try to get away from him or avoid him. And if the counsellor reproaches him for his sins, he will cover his ears with his hands and simply refuse to listen, exhibiting at the same time a look of hatred on his face. He may try to change the topic of conversation or start accusing the counsellor of being insincere and of secretly despising him. The counsellor should admit he is a burden to him. It would be better if people stopped praying for him and talking to him as it is all a complete waste of time. To avoid talking about his condition, he will accuse the counsellor of trying to blackmail him into speaking. But he is not going to be forced, otherwise he would start telling lies. The counsellor is just wasting his time and efforts, he cannot help him and so should rather turn his attention to others whom he can help. In this way the oppressed person will throw completely unfounded and imaginary accusations at the counsellor. In addition to all this he will make statements to the effect that he is a hopeless case, his desires for the world are too strong, it would be much better for him to live without all the restrictions of the Word of God. God's laws only hamper one's emotional life. His problem has nothing to do with the devil, so to command the evil forces to leave would be pointless. And it is not a matter of sin either. God made him as he is. But then he suddenly admits that he is often forced to do things against his own will. If the counsellor asks him to repeat a prayer of renunciation after him, he is either unable to pray at all or can only do so after an inner struggle. Even if he really wants to pronounce the name of Jesus, he is frequently simply unable to do so. In fact another characteristic of demonic subjection is that the condition of the oppressed person often gets worse, the more his inner agony is uncovered and the more he tries to bring the name of Christ to his lips.

However, all these and the similar statements the subjected person may express are nothing more than the 'wiles of the devil' (Eph. 6:11), who, while desiring to remain anonymous, injects his thoughts into those he has taken captive, using every imaginable lie in an attempt to sow discord and disharmony between the counsellor and the counselled. The devil's sole aim is to debase the counsellor in the eyes of the oppressed person, using all the means at his disposal to prevent his victim from hearing the voice of God, and to ultimately get him completely within his own power. Thus one finds that many people suffering from demonic subjection admit quite openly that they feel as if it is not they themselves who cherish such thoughts, but that they are rather prompted from within to talk and to act in the way they do. At a later date they may fail to understand how they were capable of such utterances and actions.

The symptoms we have just described, which mainly affect the religious attitudes of the people concerned, can psychologically either only be explained with great difficulty and in an extremely artificial manner, or not at all. In fact there is only *one* natural explanation for the utterly contradictory behaviour of these demonically oppressed and inwardly tormented people. It is, that the voice of God and the devil's voice are continually at war within them.

As an illustration of this conflict let me quote part of a letter from a demonically oppressed patient who, after a period of sustained counselling was temporarily delivered, but later suffered a relapse, and today finds herself in a state of complete inner confusion and torment.

Ex. 1. "I can't hate sin and I can't resist the devil, so

I've started going to see bad films again. I didn't want to tell you all this, because I'm afraid of you and I've not taken your advice. Please don't stop trying to help me. I get terribly unhappy thinking of all the trouble I'm causing you. I know you keep warning me, but although I want to do what you say, I still do things that are wrong. I get drawn to the pictures and into bars. You might as well stop praying for me because it's no use any more. The devil seems to say to me that it isn't as bad as all that. Such a lot of people go to these places, so why should I be so narrow-minded? God put us in the world, so why must I try and avoid everything? And yet I know I don't belong in these places. I'm not getting any better. I just get pulled backwards and forwards. I'm afraid I'll land up on the streets one day. Yet I know I'm too good for that. But anything can happen to a person, especially to me. When I can't stand the inner unrest any longer, I start drinking and smoking again. I wish I could leave these things alone. Whatever can I do? I don't pray or read my Bible any more, but I don't know why. Yet I get along all right without it. Tell me, has God given me up? I can't get back to Him by myself. Isn't there any help for me anymore? Inside I would really like to live for God and serve him. But I always fail. I'm giving up all hope. It's all useless. Why did I lack so much love when I was young and only learn to hate people? Please, help me to get out of this state again."

II. *Possession*

It is not only possible for Satan to subject people to himself, but he can also take actual possession of them. Possession is usually just a further development of demonic subjection. There is a tendency for it to occur when an oppressed person with complete disregard to his conscience heaps further guilt upon himself by, for example, subscribing himself to the devil with his own blood. But a state of possession can also result when, at the death of an already possessed person, the evil spirit leaves and enters an unbelieving descendant. In such a case the possession is not necessarily preceded by a period of demonic subjection, but may be instantaneous.

However, many people who are prepared to believe in the existence of demonic subjection deny the possibility of possession. Yet the Scriptures themselves recognize both these forms of the demonic, and distinguish clearly between them. For example we read in John 13:2 that the devil put it into the heart of Judas Iscariot to betray Jesus, and then later in the same chapter in verse 27 we find, "Then after the sop, Satan entered into Judas." For those who accept the Bible as the Word of God, there can be no doubt that during the time of Christ and the apostles, possessed people actually did exist. Furthermore, Jesus' statement that, "These signs will follow those who believe: in my name they will cast out demons", confirms the fact that possession is still a phenomenon with which we have to deal today. This is demonstrated by the fact that one can still find people, whose condition bears a striking resemblance to the recorded cases of possession in the Bible, and for which there is no other really satisfactory psychiatric or psychological explanation. However, it must be clearly stressed that possession itself, at least among civilized man, is a much rarer phenomenon than demonic subjection, and that in many instances of so-called possession one is really only dealing with a severe case of demonic subjection, or sometimes merely with the effect of a mental illness.

What then are the actual symptoms of possession? Since demonic subjection very often merges almost imperceptibly into possession, the symptoms of the latter

have much in common with the characteristics of demonic
subjection we have just been mentioning, though in the
case of possession they occur in a more intensified form.
This therefore means that it is sometimes very difficult to
distinguish between the two conditions. However, possession is frequently accompanied with the additional
symptoms of screaming, cursing, raving, grinding of
teeth, and violence. A possessed person may therefore
cause damage to objects around him, or injure himself
in an attempt to take his own life. He may also quite
frequently during a period of counselling fall into a
state of unconsciousness when the counsellor tries to
pray with him. And the same can happen during a sermon,
the outcome being that he is prevented from hearing
what is being said. A 'deaf spirit' will try to hinder him
from participating in prayer and other religious activities.
Occasionally a possessed person will emit a scornful
laugh if he hears someone talking about the cross of
Christ or the blood of Jesus. In many cases he will actually
be able to hear the devil whispering to him or even
telling him in a loud voice to act or to refrain from acting
in a certain way. At other times he may see dark figures
in his room at home. However, the demons themselves
seldom speak out of the possessed person, for their desire
is to remain unnoticed for as long as possible. It is usually
only when they are about to be driven out that they discard
their disguise and start giving expression to their fear
and horror of eviction.

In addition to the symptoms already mentioned there
are one or two other remarkable yet relatively infre-
quent phenomena associated with possession. One of
these is a trancelike state into which the possessed person
may fall, when a voice not his own speaks out of him in
a language or languages he has never learnt. On regaining
consciousness he will remember nothing of what has just
transpired. Next one finds that the possessed person

sometimes exhibits an extraordinary physical strength when in a state of rage, so much so that he must be physically restrained (Mark 5:4; Acts 19:16). Thirdly, the possessed person may exhibit powers of clairvoyance which enable him to make statements about things which humanly speaking he could never have known. He may for example just look at someone and describe their character and the sins they have committed, and accurately forecast what the future holds for them. Such statements will prove to be true as is illustrated in the case of the young girl who followed Paul and Silas at Philippi (Acts 16:16).

When one attempts to explain these extraordinary symptoms from a purely medical or parapsychological standpoint, no satisfactory solution is forthcoming. It must be immediately pointed out, however, that clairvoyance does not only occur in cases of possession, but is a faculty possessed by many other people, which although considered to be a gift by some, by the majority is recognized to be a serious burden in their lives.

Another characteristic which occurs quite frequently is the observance of strange noises, footsteps and loud knocks in the vicinity of the possessed person at night. It is not only those who are praying for the person who hear the noises, but also complete outsiders having nothing to do with the case. One finds in fact that the whole problem of ghosts and poltergeists cannot be satisfactorily explained without reference to the supernatural and the demonic.

Not infrequently one's attention is drawn to a possessed person by the evil and hateful facial expressions he adopts. This happens in particular if one talks about spiritual things in his presence, or when he is on his death bed. However, it is sometimes possible for him to mask his feelings and thereby make it very difficult for one to really appreciate his inner condition.

In addition to all that we have just mentioned, one finds that there are certain physical symptoms which occur in connection with possession. The devil may try to torment his victim by causing him to suffer pains in different parts of his body. These pains occur quite arbitrarily and bear no relationship to any known illness. They make their appearance particularly during the night with the result that the possessed person gets little or no sleep.

If a person is delivered from a state of possession his deliverance is not necessarily accompanied by any special signs. Yet the fact that deliverance has taken place can be recognized after a difficult prayer battle by the look of both happiness and release which appears upon the face of the delivered person who is now for the first time able to pronounce the name of Jesus joyfully. He will also either spontaneously or on the counsellors suggestion be immediately willing to renounce all the powers of the evil one. Moreover, the abnormal disturbances which accompanied the possession will disappear both quickly and completely. We find this to be the case with the Philippian girl whose powers of divination vanished immediately she was delivered (Acts 16:19).

In spite of everything, relapses, about which Jesus also spoke (Matt. 12:43—45), are fairly common. Thus Jesus expressly commanded the demon in the lunatic boy, "Come out of him, and never enter him again." If the delivered person receives no further counselling help, it is quite likely that his condition will degenerate into a state even worse than it was before, or he will at least become subject once more to the same form of demonic oppression.

The following excerpts are from a letter I received from a married woman, and they illustrate quite clearly a case of almost certain possession.

Ex. 2. "My marriage is very unhappy. My husband doesn't love me. He seems to be going his own way more and more. My marriage is just a long path of suffering. Yet I regard it as a means of fellowship with my Lord's sufferings which leads me into a closer communion with Him ... My husband is almost always restless and has no peace of mind. The smallest setback makes him lose control ... Our daughter is never as difficult as when her father is at home. My husband's presence is sometimes almost unbearable because something evil seems to exude from him. He can't stand me being with him either. It often appears to me as though evil wants to break out of him at the slightest opportunity. He quarrels for no reason at all. He shouts out harshly, slams the doors, yet continually justifies his actions and ridicules anything that is good. I can't believe anything he says, because I never know whether or not he is telling the truth. Often when he looks at me, his expression is cold and evil. Whenever he argues, he always contradicts himself. Yet with other people he appears almost unnaturally polite and good-natured. And he even comes to church with me sometimes, although he never remembers what the sermon was about. But if he says grace at table or sings a chorus, he just does it mechanically; his mind seems to be miles away. He's cynical about the hymns in the hymn book. He never feels any guilt, but is always accusing others and is discontent with our situation in life. And then he's often telling other people bad things about me, but I don't say anything, in order to keep the peace.

For some time now our house has been haunted. At night we hear footsteps and knocking and grinding noises coming from the loft. And when I get down on my knees to pray, there are knocks in the room itself. In the morning also when I read my Bible I can sometimes hear steps and knocking overhead. Our daughter has also been disturbed during the night by these noises. Once when I wanted to fetch my hymn book, I definitely sensed that something was sitting on the couch looking at me with the same evil expression my husband sometimes has on his face. When I prayed out loud, though, and asked Jesus to protect us and our house, a great sense of joy came over me. And the house has been quieter since then. We still hear the 'spirit' though, particularly if my husband gets into one of his states and begins to be abusive. But it doesn't frighten me any more, because when I thank Jesus for having overcome all the powers of darkness, the noises subside. It's the same when I pray out loud while the knocking is going on. It disappears for a while. When my husband went away once, the noises disappeared completely and only started again when he came back home. Once when I was praying, the pages of my Bible were suddenly turned over by what seemed like and invisible hand, and I felt a cold breath of air go past me. Yet the doors and windows were closed. Quite recently my daughter who sleeps in the room next to mine, heard someone walking about in my room while I was fast asleep. There's definitely something going on in our house. My husband's continual restlessness is a source of great sorrow to me, particularly since he is also tormented by thoughts of committing suicide . . . ."

Since in this example the wife's description of her husband's behaviour pattern is in itself sufficient to indicate a probable case of possession, the additional information concerning the haunting and other ghostlike phenomena leaves us in little doubt about the matter.

C. THE DISTINCTION BETWEEN DISEASE AND THE DEMONIC

The question facing us now is, what are the actual differences between disease and the demonic? Is there any coincidence between the symptoms of demonic subjection and possession we have already mentioned, and the typical symptoms of psychiatric illnesses, or is the coincidence only partial?

I. *Schizophrenia or the Demonic?*

Let us first of all take a quick look at the typical characteristics of schizophrenia.

In its earlier stages this illness is particularly difficult to distinguish from demonic subjection, since schizophrenia and the demonic on the surface at least have much in common. One can understand therefore why a number of mistakes are made in diagnosis, especially since many Christian workers are prone to label any form of mental illness as an expression of the demonic, and since many psychiatrists regard possession as a type of mental illness. And yet at times a psychiatrist will meet a case he is unable to accommodate satisfactorily within the usual framework of schizophrenic illnesses, which therefore leaves a question mark over his actual diagnosis.

Now an impartial observer might suspect that a case of schizophrenia was actually a case of demonic subjection if a teenager for example, showing no signs of abnormality, should suddenly rebel against his parents, become stubborn, ill-natured, excitable and unsociable, react violently against his environment and begin to act in a quite unpredictable manner. The same might be true in the case of a young man who for apparently no reason at all begins to suffer from states of anxiety and depressions which, in his own words, come upon him like a black cloud attempting to crush him to death. He may believe at times that he must hang himself, or he may kneel down in the most awkward situations and pray out loud in order to repel the enemy who is trying to attack him. In a similar way it seems reasonable at first sight to believe that the demonic plays some part when a person is absolutely convinced that he has demons living within him, and that they are the cause of his physical ailments, or when a person feels he is being harassed by a demon, or has been hypnotized or bewitched, and when he continually tells his friends that some foreign power compels him to think and to act in the way he does.

However, all these signs and more besides, are very often the typical symptoms of a schizophrenic illness. It is almost invariably true to say that if a person is for ever talking about being possessed, he is really suffering from some form of mental illness rather than from a demonic influence. This opinion seems to be confirmed by the fact that with people like this one usually observes a gradual deterioration of the personality taking place in conjunction with an ever increasing number of manias and delusions. If such is the case, there can be no doubt at all that the problem is one of schizophrenia with the associated mania of possession. That the patient's delusions have a demonic flavour is probably the result of his having read or heard something concerning demons or the demonic either before or at the onset of his illness. Even when a person claims he is hearing strange noises, or is seeing weird apparitions, these must only be regarded as either auditory or visual hallucinations, especially if his associates experience none of these phenomena.

The delusion of possession can completely dominate a mentally ill person. Due to the relative frequency of this condition, the following example will aid us in gaining a better insight into the problem.

Ex. 3. A 30-year-old patient at the beginning of her treatment told me that she was demon possessed. She put this down to the fact that she had been treated by a mesmeriser earlier in her life. The man had made a strange impression on her and had talked with her about spirit-

istic meetings and seances. Later she had heard and read
about the sinister results that can issue from this type
of treatment. As a result of this she became depressed
and tired of living and was gripped by a paralysing
feeling of oppression and fear. Then, only three years
prior to our talk, she joined a Free Church, but had
subsequently started experiencing some peculiar sensations in her body. On the advice of her minister she
prayed a prayer of renunciation but this had only caused
it, according to her own words, to whistle around inside
her head like a whirlwind. At her baptism as she received
the benediction, the devil seemed to start throwing her
backwards and forwards, so much so that she could not
kneel down. Once when a visiting speaker was at the
church she had had to run outside and scream. Because
of this the speaker had thought it necessary to drive
the demon out of her, and after the attempt had been
made, she felt better for a while. Later, however, she had
felt a definite knocking in her right arm which she thought
showed that the demon had not completely left. The
following night something large and heavy had been laid
upon her chest, but the sensation had disappeared when
she prayed, although it later returned. The next evening
something like a flock of ravens had flown towards her
and she had also seen some black owls. She had been
continually thumped and hit while in bed, and on another
night she had had her head pushed forward by an unseen
force. Once when she was wide awake, she saw a man
in shirt sleeves with an evil looking face standing at the
end of her bed. The demon also often assaulted her
sexually. This she experienced through a distinct tingling
sensation at night, which made it impossible for her to
know how to lie down or how to defend herself. She also
felt this sensation during the day sometimes, particularly
when she wanted to pray. The devil had also spoken to
her once and said, "You have blasphemed against the

Holy Spirit! Love your neighbour as you love yourself! Give up the ghost!" She had heard the voice speaking within her somewhat in the same way as one sees with the imagination. On another occasion she had felt as if something had flown down from her head, and then a kind of battle had broken out inside her. Then she had suddenly regained contact with God. People, she said, might think she was mentally ill, but her friends knew otherwise and she was quite normal. Once a voice had called out of her, "You poor trapped human being," but as she thought of the fact that Jesus was with her she had suddenly felt a ray of light strike her and had known that an angel of God was there fighting against Satan. On reading the words in the Bible, "His mercy endures for ever," it had become bright and warm within her. That, she claimed, was Jesus. It was as if a hand had taken hold of her heart. One night she had seen Jesus with her own eyes sitting in the clouds looking down at her. His eyes had suddenly been filled with love towards her and she had known she had nothing to fear. Visions of this nature were frequent. Later a second attempt had been made to cast the demon out of her, this time by a Christian woman, but she had felt the enemy putting up a terrible struggle, like a bumble bee buzzing around inside. Although the woman had said she was now deliv- ered, the buzzing had continued and she had suffered new attacks. The year before, for two whole months she had inwardly stunk like the plague, and while talking to me she still claimed that she often felt the buzzing inside, together with strong currents in various parts of her body. And the tingling continued to plague her at night. She could not concentrate enough to pray, because she was still bound. She could not work, because she was always tired and unable to remember things. Sometimes when she wanted to pray, she would start hearing swear words, and she often could not even pronounce the name of

Jesus. After a third attempt to drive the demon out, the electric currents in her body had decreased for a while, only to return later to their previous intensity. During a morning service at the church she had suddenly started to tremble all over. She felt as if the demon inside her had leant forward and shaken his fist furiously at the speaker. Lately the people at the church had started doubting that it was really a case of possession. This made her sad, because she knew the devil really wanted people to believe she was mentally ill so that he would be left in peace.

These were only some of the woman's numerous complaints. She never tired of talking about all her abnormal thoughts and feelings. Even though initially some of the remarks she made might have suggested some demonic influence, as she went on talking it soon became apparent that she was suffering from schizophrenia. The incoherent, strange and eccentric ideas and experiences, the auditory and visual hallucinations, the continual affirmation that demons were living within her, were without doubt of a morbid nature. With genuine cases of possession one finds no such ideas or sensations. The messages she received came not from angels or demons, but originated from within her own sick mind. In a case like this therefore, it would be wrong to accept all the patient's statements concerning the indwelling evil spirits at their face value, for if one did so, it would only serve to strengthen the person's actual delusion.

With Christians, schizophrenia almost always appears in a religious guise. The sick person will believe that his Christian life has been damaged by Satan on account of the terrible feeling of unrest which fills and robs him of his peace and desire to pray. The darkness within him he explains by saying that God has forsaken him and evil powers have taken control. He feels cut off from the Holy Spirit and he can no longer hear Christ's voice.

He cannot even pronounce the name of Jesus now, no matter how much he wants to. He dreams about the most absurd things and yet attaches a great importance to them. For a while he may feel extremely happy as a Christian and speak exuberantly about his faith, but later he starts crying aloud as a feeling of complete despair overwhelms him. Because he finds the most simple of tasks beyond him, he is soon forced to resign from his job, but if his friends tell him he is suffering from some illness, he vehemently denies this.

Ex. 4. A young man wrote to me once, "One evening a year ago when I was just about to go to sleep, having read my Bible and prayed, a terrible swear word suddenly came into my mind. At the same time I felt as if something left me and I thought I was going to die. I jumped out of bed and started walking around the room, but the feeling persisted. It was just as if the Holy Spirit had flown away from me. I started to tremble, so I took my Bible, fell on my knees and prayed for forgiveness. Yet a terrible feeling of unrest gripped me and it still grips me today. Things have become a lot worse now than at the beginning. I went to see my doctor and then a psychiatrist, after which I was admitted to a psychiatric clinic. They treated me with drugs and gave me electro-convulsive therapy and I stayed there for several months, but I'm still convinced that I'm lost. Please write and tell me if I am going to hell. Almost all the time the most unimaginable swear words and curses well up inside me. (He then quoted in his letter more than a dozen such words.) My joy has completely gone and I am filled with fear and anxiety all the time now. I find it extremely difficult to do the simplest of tasks. But I've never dabbled in occultism, nor have my parents. I had such a lot of joy as a Christian. And now I've lost all my assurance and peace. The worst thing is that it's all my own fault. Hebrews 10:26—31 applies to me perfectly. Yet people tell me this isn't true, but I simply can't believe anything else. It must refer to me. I've thought recently it would be best to commit suicide. Will I ever get better again?...."

Ex. 5. Another patient of mine up till the time of his illness had been living a sound Christian life, but he had gradually become filled with the terrible fear of being eternally damned. His moods, however, would suddenly change and for a while he would experience a joy he had never felt before. Once a voice which he took to be the voice of God had commanded him to get onto a tram and sing the gospel to the passengers. On another occasion he jumped out of bed in the middle of the night, threw himself on his knees and cried to God for mercy since he felt he was about to be thrown into hell. Next he imagined that he was in fact the Antichrist and was calling to Satan for help in his rebellion against God. He often believes he is being persecuted by evil spirits. Allegedly he can feel the devil at work in his own body. The proof that demons are already living within him is the strong burning sensation he keeps feeling. Quite innocent events are interpreted as being the result of occult attacks. Every attempt to reason with him and to persuade him to seek medical help fails. He will only accept someone's advice if they agree with him that he is possessed. However, an attempt at exorcism only served to worsen his condition. It has become more and more obvious even to those with no medical training that he is really suffering from a mental illness.

It should be pointed out though, that demonic subjection and mental illness often occur simultaneously. This we can illustrate by means of another brief example.

Ex. 6. The patient's ancestors had practised charming, his mother had been an alcoholic, his sister had died in a mental institution and the patient himself was somewhat addicted to alcohol. His job was that of an unqualified medical practitioner, and by using a pendulum he was able to give accurate information concerning dead and missing people. As time went on though, he gradually began to suffer from a persecution mania, the intensity of which continued to increase in spite of the fact that it was completely unfounded. About this time he came into contact with a certain evangelist who after an authoritative counselling session with him released him from the demonic ban over his life. Nevertheless the persecution mania continued and his relatives were forced to the conclusion that he was in fact suffering from a form of mental illness.

This is a typical case of endogenous mental illness. However, the added complication of demonic oppression, the result of the occult practices of his forefathers, was apparent on account of his pendulum ability, his frequent swearing and his cynical attitude towards religious matters.

However, not only are many cases of schizophrenia regarded as instances of possession, but the reverse is also true, and it is not unusual to find an actual case of possession being regarded as merely a form of mental illness. For example, anyone exhibiting today the symptoms of the Gadarene demoniac mentioned in Mark 5, would almost certainly be admitted to a psychiatric institute and diagnosed as suffering from a mental illness. His screams and nakedness, his self-inflicted injuries and violence are all to be found in fact among the symptoms of certain cases of severe mental illness. However, the fact that he was actually possessed is revealed not only by his rapid deliverance following Jesus' command for the demons to leave, but also by the strange voice issuing from him and saying, "What have you to do with me, Jesus, Son of the Most High? I adjure you by God, do not torment me." In contrast to this, the utterances of the troubled mental patient will simply consist of a series of illogical and nonsensical statements which he may continue to repeat to himself for hours, or he may from time to time hold conversations with figures that appear to him, using the most weird expressions and uttering the most absurd ideas. This will at once cancel out the possibility of possession, for a possessed person, though he may be restless and even driven into a rage at times, will nevertheless remain sane in his thoughts.

One can therefore say: a mentally ill person is in fact still ill, even when he exhibits certain symptoms characteristic of possession. On the other hand a possessed person is in fact mentally healthy in spite of the fact that at intervals he may exhibit certain symptoms of mental abnormality. In additition to this it is noticeable that the mentally ill will usually give expression to their thoughts quite fervently, whereas a possessed person will often do so only after much hesitation, and then only if he is urged to speak. While the mental patient will speak in extravagant tones of the demons he alleges to be living inside himself, the possessed person avoids all mention of demons as long as no one approaches him on a spiritual level. In this way the evil spirit prevents his victim from betraying his presence.

It is also likely to be a case of mental illness if the person concerned until the time of his illness was living a sound and healthy Christian life, and if instead of a history of occult oppression in the family, there is a history of mental and emotional illness. Furthermore, if he displays no signs of opposition to any form of Christian counselling, or just listens indifferently and remains unmoved when people attempt to exorcise the demons, or if he finds no difficulty in pronouncing the name of Jesus, all this is indicative of mental illness rather than the demonic. If a person is really possessed, he will fight and struggle against prayer and all other forms of Christian influences he comes into contact with, since the demons will do their utmost to avoid being thrown out of their home. Thus any pronounced resistance exhibited during times of counselling would suggest immediately the possibility that the demonic is involved.

One particular symptom that frequently calls forth varied interpretations is the hearing of voices. The uninformed usually connect this at once with the presence of evil forces. And yet this phenomenon is to be observed much more frequently with schizophrenics than with possessed people. The voices which a patient says originate from strange people who talk about him, watch him, assault him and persecute him, are usually always of a pathological nature. These voices often command him to do things completely out of character as for example to run away, to stop eating, to commit suicide, and so on. And yet he feels he has to obey them. And then when he really wants to do something of his own free will, the voices prevent him. Moreover the words the mentally ill person hears are often completely nonsensical. In general it is true to say that if a person suffers from delusions as well as hears voices, he is a victim of some mental disease.

The satanic voices heard by a possessed person are of a completely different nature. From the psychological point of view they are quite understandable, for they feed the person's mind with ideas opposed to the Christian faith. For example he may possibly hear a voice saying to him, "You've got a great calling, but don't believe there's a God. What you hear from the Bible and the counsellor is nonsense. Praying can't help you and you won't get away from me, because you are mine. Kill yourself." The source of these voices can be some frightening apparition that the possessed person senses or even sees around him. One of my patients who had dabbled in occultism earlier in her life, after her father had died saw him almost every night and talked with him just as if he were a real person. Another patient who had subscribed herself to the devil, frequently heard voices forbidding her to take the counsellor's advice, and threatening her with violence if she told anyone else about what she heard. Moreover she often saw the devil standing in front of herself, telling her she had to belong to him and saying that if she surrendered her life to Christ, he would punish her on account of the sins she had committed. In general then, if the voices are demonic in origin they will attempt to lure the person away from God, whereas if they are the result of some mental abnormality they will merely speak of unnatural and nonsensical things.

One must be very careful when listening to the relatives of a schizophrenic if they affirm that the patient is obviously possessed because he has dabbled in occultism earlier in his life, and one must be particularly on guard when the patient himself claims he is being influenced by strange people around him. It is undoubtedly true that occult practices can trigger off some forms of mental disturbance. However, in practice one finds much more frequently that the mental illness in question has some typical endogenous cause, which has nothing to do with occult bondage.

II. *Epilepsy or the Demonic?*

The next question we must ask is whether or not it is possible to arrive at a satisfactory conclusion concerning the origin of epileptic fits. A number of Christian workers are inclined to the view that all cases of epilepsy and almost all other instances of unconsciousness are indicative of the demonic. They base their argument on the biblical account of the 'lunatic' boy out of whom Jesus drove an evil spirit. However, in order to prove that an epileptic is suffering from some demonic influence, one would have to demonstrate the presence of one of the underlying causes we outlined at the very beginning of our discussion. However, in most cases this cannot be proved. And besides, one can find a number of Christians who in spite of suffering from epilepsy live sound and healthy Christian lives. One would also have to explain why, if epilepsy were always of a demonic nature, certain drugs can often effect an improvement in the patient's condition. It seems to me that in the case of the 'lunatic' boy, he had been possessed from childhood and the possession had manifested itself in the form of an epileptic fit. These fits were probably instigated by the demon in an attempt to detroy him. In fact the ultimate aim of the evil powers is always to kill the one they possess, and to deliver him into the hands of Satan. Thus for example the boy's father exclaimed, "It often casts him into the fire and into the water to destroy him" (Mark 9:22). Indeed, even as the spirit was about to be driven out it tore and convulsed the boy again in a final attempt to take his life.

Yet epilepsy does not only appear in the form of fits and similar lapses of consciousness, but also manifests itself in recurrent periods of ill-humour which occur every two or three weeks and which last for one or two days at a time. The change in personality is usually perceptible first thing in the morning but without apparent cause. The person becomes morose, bad-tempered and moody, and wants to be left alone. He gets angry, critical and abusive over the smallest trifle, and gives vent to filthy expressions, quarrels and even becomes violent at times. Or on the other hand he may despair of life and contemplate committing suicide. In general he will remain lucid in his thinking although occasionally his mind may become clouded and he may lapse into a state of semiconsciousness after which he will remember nothing of his previous behaviour. Between attacks a person in this state will be thoroughly amenable to conversation on matters of religion and the Christian faith.

The fact that the condition we have just described gives an impression of the demonic to some people is understandable. However, it would be quite unjustified to assume that this was the case, especially if the pattern of electrical activity in the brain was indicative of epilepsy. It is therefore inexcusable and sometimes quite disastrous to find certain Christian workers labelling almost all cases of epilepsy, unconsciousness and fits as symptoms of demonic subjection.

III. *Mental Depression or the Demonic?*

Let us now go on to consider the subject of mental depression or melancholia, as it is sometimes called. There are a number of Christian counsellors who advocate the idea that melancholia is always a symptom of either demonic oppression or possession. And indeed there does seem to be a strong argument in support of this particular point of view, in so far that at the height of his depression a patient is often unable to accept either the Word of God or the fact of his own salvation, and refuses to believe in the possibility of forgiveness and assurance. Instead, he believes that his heart has been hardened and that he may even be possessed, because he finds it impossible to concentrate both when praying and when reading his Bible. However, rather than being a sign of actual alienation from God, these symptoms are typical of the morbid thoughts associated with melancholia. It would therefore again be foolish to give credence to the patient's conviction that he is possessed. He is far more likely to be suffering from some morbid delusion. This becomes apparent when one notices that those who believe themselves to be possessed are usually simultaneously plagued with other delusions as for example of having committed an unpardonable sin, or of being persecuted and talked about by others, or of being poverty stricken, or of suffering from some incurable disease, all of which prove to be completely unfounded. Experience shows that as in the case of schizophrenics, a person who continually talks about being possessed is in fact deluding himself. On the contrary, a person who is really possessed will never let the idea of possession enter his head, even if there is no other explanation for his condition. As we have already said, this is Satan's method of remaining undetected. One finds quite often that even in the case of mental depressives who have previously dabbled in occultism and who blame this for their so-called possession, prior to their illness they have been living sound, healthy and well-balanced Christian lives which in itself is a good indication that they have not succumbed to some sudden demonic attack. It is therefore wrong to associate mental depression with the demonic just because the patient experiences moods of despondency and despair. A heart filled with hatred and darkness, however, presents another picture.

Now one also finds innumerable counsellors taking the view that the blasphemous thoughts which arise in the mind of the mental depressive are a sure sign of the demonic. In fact the following statement actually occurs in a widely circulated book of a well-known evangelist: "If a person suffers from blasphemous thoughts, it is almost certain that he has been charmed, perhaps as a child, and has now fallen under the spell of the devil." This conclusion, however, is completely unfounded as far as mental depressives are concerned, and this must be made absolutely clear to people, for otherwise a great and terrible injustice will be done to those who while suffering from melancholia, are at the same time plagued with blasphemous thoughts. One finds that Christians who fall victim to mental depression are particularly prone to such thoughts. If this is so, then the thoughts must be regarded as pathological delusions. In the case of over-conscientious and anxious melancholic patients, thoughts of this nature often arise out of a fear of blaspheming against the Holy Spirit. Here the psychological law applies that what is feared often occurs. Quite frequently therefore when these people read the Bible, or pray, or go to church, or to a communion service, blasphemous thoughts arise as a direct result of their fear of blaspheming. This has nothing to do with some devilish influence, which is demonstrated by the fact that the thoughts disappear when the person is cured of his melancholia. If the thoughts had really been symptomatic of the demonic, medical treatment alone would not have eliminated them. The picture is quite different, however, if the blasphemous thoughts appear in conjunction with cursing in the life of a person who puts little store by religion and who exhibits no symptoms of mental depression. In fact if the person has had any contact with occultism or has been guilty of gross sin, the demonic origin of his thoughts is almost indisputable.

One can therefore establish the rule that if blasphemous thoughts arise within a person's heart and are consciously expressed without the slightest remorse, they will in almost every case have been prompted by the devil. On the other hand, if the thoughts force themselves upon the person, and instead of being expressed are abhorred and genuinely repented of, they will most likely be of a pathological nature. A demonically affected person will care little about his blasphemous thoughts, but the mental depressive will lament the fact that he is capable of thinking such things. Such a person may even be unable to pronounce the name of Jesus for fear of having to blaspheme or to slander his name. On the other hand, if the demonically oppressed are prevented from mentioning

Jesus' name, it is as a result of their hatred and abhorrence of it.

There is likewise a fundamental difference between the underlying causes of the suicidal tendencies of demonically oppressed and mentally depressed people. The demonically oppressed person as a result of the devil's promptings can even want to kill himself. It is a completely conscious action on his own part as we have already mentioned, for which he must bear full responsibility. On the other hand with the mental depressive the suicidal thoughts arise primarily out of the overpowering pathologically based conviction that he has committed unforgivable sins. The patient's weariness of life is utilized by Satan to tempt him to kill himself. If he succeeds in committing suicide it is because his mind has been blinded and his reason destroyed. He is thus not responsible for his own actions at such a time.

The following example will help us understand a little of the very real problem concerning suicide and the mentally depressed or melancholic Christian.

Ex. 7. A minister in his forties came from a much afflicted family. His mother, two of his uncles, and one of his brothers were all mental depressives. Yet one could find no occult prehistory in the family. From a very early age the patient had been a very serious and easily depressed person who had kept himself to himself. His strict upbringing had been the source of little joy to him as a child, and then on account of a mistake he made when he was eighteen, and in spite of genuine repentance, he found himself plagued with the memory of his deed. He suffered his first real depression just after he had completed his theological studies. This was accompanied by a terrible anxiety concerning his ability to preach, since he felt he was neither worthy nor gifted enough for this task. He had then married, and his wife had been exceedingly sympathetic towards her husband's mental affliction. They had had two children. His ministry had caused him a great deal of concern and he began to brood a lot and spend hours over the preparation of his sermons. He continually reproached himself and suffered terribly from an inferiority complex, a feeling of apathy, a lack of will power, and thoughts of suicide. On top of all this his wife developed a serious heart complaint. As the years went by, he found that he spent more and more time receiving medical treatment on account of his severe mental depressions, the treatment often lasting for several months at a time. He was convinced that he would never be cured and this in itself was a great source of anxiety to him. But in spite of everything he knew himself to be a child of God and never doubted the Lord's power to help him. However, since his prayers were apparently so often unanswered, his burden only increased. He once wrote, "My cries fall on deaf ears. The worst thing is that when I am depressed, although I can read the Bible and pray for hours, I find no satisfaction or strength in doing so. But I know and believe that God won't leave me."

One evening he was attacked again by a terrible feeling of fear and restlessness. He got in contact with another Christian counsellor and had a long talk with him. Later he wrote several letters to settle the affairs of his life. He then killed himself. He left the letters in his study together with a hymn book open at the hymn 'Jesus accepts sinners'.

The people in the village where he lived were not able to understand how a minister could take his own life. If he had practised what he preached from the pulpit, he would never have done this, they thought. When his wife too began to exhibit signs of melancholia as a result of the terrible experiences she had had to go through, the parishioners started asking themselves whether it was contagious. In fact the majority of them said quite simply that she had inherited the evil spirit which had been in her husband, particularly when she also began to think of committing suicide. They could see no other explanation for it. It just had to be the devil's influence. The non-Christians in the village on the other hand said quite simply, that this was the result of being too religious. The minister's death and his depressions were criticized from the purely moral point of view, and it was assumed that because he had written the letters just before his death, he must have been in complete control of his senses when he had actually killed himself, and this they just could not understand.

The reaction of the villagers is a clear indication of the wide-spread ignorance concerning mental depression. We have already seen that many of the battles going on in a person's mind must really be regarded as a symptom of mental illness. As the intensity of the illness increases, the patient is sometimes attacked by vivid delusions and it is often impossible to persuade him from them. He frequently believes that God has forsaken him on account of his sins which he sees ever before his eyes, and he thus considers himself to be eternally damned. He may be completely dominated by the thought of committing suicide, feeling that this is the only way he can atone for his sins. He gradually becomes irrational in his thinking, and is therefore no longer responsible for his subsequent attempts to kill himself. He is in a state of mental confusion. This state can arise very quickly, sometimes with the result that one moment the patient is capable of intelligent conversation and the next moment the thought of committing suicide has overwhelmed him. Proof of this is the fact that many patients who fail in their attempt are later unable to explain why they acted in the way they did. Indeed, they may only remember what has happened very vaguely, and they are usually

also unaware of the fact that Satan is using their illness
as a means of ending their life. We have to accept the fact
that God in His wisdom allows the enemy to induce a
person to commit suicide without holding the person
responsible for his action. God's ways are not our ways
and His thoughts not our thoughts. So although we
are often unable to understand why He allows these
things to happen, it is sufficient to know that, "From
him and through him and to him are all things" (Rom.
11:33—36). We are never in a position therefore to
judge a person whose actions we find beyond our
understanding.

If the evil spirits, however, believe that through in-
ducing the patient to commit suicide they are delivering
him up to Satan, then they are sadly mistaken. The
Christian can be in no doubt at all that this is only allowed
by God, because He knows that rather than the person
falling into Satan's hands, he falls in fact into the open
arms of his Saviour. We can be utterly certain that God in
his unlimited mercy will accept the faith of the mental
depressive and welcome him into his kingdom, where
tears and pain and sorrow and mourning shall be no
more, and that He will pay no regard to actions for
which a person is not responsible. If prior to his illness
the patient was living close to his Lord, his salvation
will never be in jeopardy, even if as a result of his illness
he has taken his own life, for if this happens, God
will judge him according to the faith he possessed before
his illness. His suicide is only an apparent victory for
the evil one, for the real victory still belongs to the
Lord Jesus.

However, we must underline the fact that what we
have just been saying applies only in the case of
endogenous melancholia, and not in the case of reactive
or psychopathic depressions in which the patient, in spite
of being plagued with suicidal thoughts, still remains in

complete control of his senses and is therefore still responsible for his actions.

The type of melancholia we have just been describing is sometimes utilized by Satan as an open door through which to launch his attacks, for the mental and emotional resistance of the person suffering from this disease is automatically lowered. When this is the case the patient will not only reproach himself but will also begin to vehemently complain about his relatives and friends, and will start criticizing God as well. Again the compulsion to commit suicide will well up within him as the devil persuades him that he has no hope and is lost.

However, there is a distinct difference between this condition and the mental pressure experienced by a demonically oppressed person. In such a case the pressure results from either some gross sin committed by the person himself, or from his own or his ancestors involvement in occultism. The depressions experienced by a person in this condition will be marked by a terrible feeling of fear and unrest, accompanied by fits of anger and a defiance and aversion for everything to do with God or the Christian faith.

It is quite obvious therefore that each case of mental depression demands a very detailed investigation of the patient's moral and occult history. Unless this is done one will be unable to arrive at a clear understanding of the patient's problem.

As an illustration of this I will quote the following example in which it is very difficult to answer the question, mental depression or the demonic.

Ex. 8. The patient's great-grandfather had suffered a great deal from depressions and had exhibited suicidal tendencies. Her grandfather had hanged himself while under the influence of drink. Her father's moods had affected the whole family, and sometimes for weeks he had never spoken to them and had continually threatened to shoot himself. With visitors, however, he had always been apparently extremely sociable, although his most usual topics of conversation had consisted of glass moving, table-lifting, card laying, necromancy, using a pendulum, and so on. The patient herself had personally participated in all these occult activities without being conscious of the dangers involved. Her grandmother on her father's side who had been a midwife, had often cast spells on animals and people. The patient herself had been held over some smoldering herbs when she was a child in an attempt to heal her of a skin disease, and when this had failed, she had been taken to another woman and charmed after which she had been cured.

Ever since childhood she had had a shy and depressed nature which combined with a continual feeling of loneliness had forced her to lock herself in her room at times and talk to herself. She had also been very impressionable, and as a teenager had gone along with one of her girl friends to see a fortune-teller. The fortune-teller had told her about things she could not possibly have known in any ordinary way, and had also accurately prophesied her future. She had had a very strict upbringing and had often been beaten by her father. Because her mother had tried to intervene once, her father had beaten the mother unconscious in front of the daughter's very eyes and dragged her downstairs by her hair. She therefore from a very early age developed a fear of her father which later turned to hatred, particularly when he was unfaithful to her mother. She also continued to suffer a great deal from loneliness and found it impossible to talk to either of her parents.

She was 25 when she first tried to commit suicide as a result of some difficulties she met in her job. She was at once admitted to a psychiatric clinic, but a few years later following her mother's death she again attempted to kill herself. This time she was accepted into a Christian sanatorium and there she became a real Christian. Her depressions immediately abated a little, one reason being that she became friendly with another Christian girl. However, later on she again had to pass through some severe depressions which made her feel bitter inside and angry against God, and which caused her to lose all the reality of her faith and forgiveness. The desire to take her own life returned and even today she finds it difficult sometimes to get it out of her mind. During her depressions she found it almost impossible to read her Bible or to pray, and she felt as if a massive wall was between herself and God. Her feeling of utter hopelessness and despair would make her start accusing God. In conjunction with this it seemed as if a great abyss would open up between herself and other people, and she would feel misunderstood, despised and rejected by all her friends, so much so that she would distrust everyone.

On the other hand when she was free from depression she was filled with a deep love for God and was conscious that her sins had been forgiven. Prayer and Bible reading were an essential part of her life, together with church attendance and the hearing of the Word of God. Thus in spite of the much suffering she had to endure and overcome, she had a great joy in working for her Lord.

Following a period of counselling during which she renounced the works of the devil, in spite of a considerable improvement in her condition she still found it very difficult to speak at meetings about her faith although in the course of her job she found it easy to talk to people. She finds that she can only overcome this strong feeling of inadequacy after she has received further counselling and encouragement.

The underlying root of the problem here seems to be a considerable endogenous predisposition towards depressiveness which has resulted in a form of melancholia, that in turn has been coloured by a severe case of occult oppression. The patient had experienced this demonic subjection for a number of years following her conversion, but as a result of her giving her life afresh to Christ and of the counsellor praying a prayer of renunciation with her and loosing her from the ban of her ancestors, the oppression was apparently almost completely overcome. However, her inability to speak about her faith indicates that her deliverance is probably not absolute, and she is very likely correct in believing that this is the devil's way in keeping her from fulfilling God's will for her life.

IV. *Neuroses or the Demonic?*

We now have to turn our attention to those mental disturbances which appear to be conditioned by certain experiences in the past life of the patient, namely neuroses. Many emotionally sensitive people as a result of some troubling experience or stress in their lives, completely lose their powers of reason and subsequently react in all sorts of morbid ways. They may exhibit for example a great deal of fear and restlessness, or may burst out crying, and start screaming and lamenting, or they may run away, fall into a state of stupor, see visions, or suffer all manner of bodily complaints. Again it is all too easy to come to the hasty conclusion that there is something demonic lurking behind the patient's troubles. Yet a detailed investigation of his mental life usually reveals that what was at first sight inexplicable or ascribed to the devil has in fact a typical psychological cause.

One therefore usually finds that alleged visions of the devil, of angels, or of Christ, are emotionally conditioned hallucinations stemming from some irrational fear or wish fulfillment of the patient.

Ex. 9. A woman who had a continual death wish, one night saw Death standing beside her bed in the form of a skeleton. This resulted in a terrible fear of the devil and the Last Judgement building up inside her, so much so that on another night she had a vision of Satan coming to her and trying to take her away. Yet the demonic played no part in her condition, for after the underlying causes of her illness had been explained to her, the visions disappeared once and for all.

As well as satanically inspired visions and those resulting from mental ill-health, emotional instability can also be responsible for phenomena of this nature. However, these three types of hallucinations are quite distinct from one another. The following example is another illustration of emotionally conditioned visions.

Ex. 10. A Christian girl suffered from states of anxiety, an inner unrest, and an inability to either read her Bible or pray. In addition to this she quite often saw dark apparitions around her which used to accuse her. Thinking herself to be possessed, she despaired of life. A Christian worker untrained in psychology would most likely have also thought her to be possessed, and would have therefore acted on this assumption. However, an analysis of her subconscious revealed quite definitely that her condition was to be traced back to one particular event in her past life. The girl had once known a woman who had talked to her about evil spirits and told her that some of these spirits would transfer themselves over to her and bring misfortune into her life. Since the girl was emotionally very sensitive, the woman's prophecy had affected her a great deal, and she had been filled with a feeling of immense fear. When the cause of her fears was brought to the surface though and explained to her, she was completely cured. This was proof enough that she had never been possessed but only gripped by a pathological fear.

Innumerable people have come to me with their various fears, anxieties and depressions. Through having had

contact with some allegedly possessed person they feel
burdened, and fear there may have been some transference
of the occult powers on to themselves. Many believe that
they are actually already possessed. But since when a
person believes himself to be possessed it can be ascer-
tained that the problem is really one of neurosis, the
patient can be told with confidence that his fears are
unfounded. If he can be persuaded to accept this fact,
his fear and anxiety disappear immediately.

Similarly, states of stupor and semiconsciousness are
also more than likely to be the result of some mental
trouble, and thus they can usually be regarded as a type
of hysterical illness. The patient either consciously or
unconsciously slips into this state of apparent self-
hypnosis in order to withdraw from reality and thereby
escape into a dream-world of his own. Once the actual
reason for this withdrawal is discovered, his condition
rapidly improves. However, certain semiconscious states
I believe are definitely caused by the demonic. For example, on several occasions I have seen a possessed
person begin to scream and to rage about, or tear a Bible
up and laugh derisively when someone has spoken to
him of Christ. One finds that the person is oblivious to
his own behaviour, for later he remembers nothing of
what has happened. This was true in the case of Gottliebin
Dittus, a possessed girl who was counselled by the well-
known German Lutheran minister Blumhardt; and Dr.
Koch himself had the same experience with the possessed
Philippino boy he counselled in Indonesia. The story is
described in his book 'Unter der Führung Jesu'. In the
latter example a demonic state of semiconsciousness occurred time and time again while the Christians were
praying for the boy. One finds therefore that while
psychogenetic semiconscious states originating from the
subconscious mind can be interrupted by outside influences, demonic stupors, produced and used by the

devil to serve his own ends, are usually so deep that it is not possible to awaken the person. In the case of spiritistic mediums, their trances must be considered to be partly demonic and partly psychological in nature.

Then again, if a very sensitive and anxious type of person who has heard people talking about ghosts starts hearing knocking noises himself, one is almost certainly dealing with another form of neurosis. For example when a certain patient of mine started thinking about her father who had died in unbelief, she would hear strange noises during the night. However, other people living in the house failed to hear the noises, and it turned out that the patient was actually afraid of her father's spirit being transferred to her and had started imagining the noises because of this.

Although many conditions having a form similar to that of demonic subjection ultimately prove to be of a purely neurotic nature, one finds on the other hand that many apparent neuroses can be traced back to the demonic. The following is an example of this.

Ex. 11. A 40-year-old spinster suffered a lot from recurring states of depression and irritability. At such times she was plagued by a great feeling of restlessness and even by temporary fits of rage in which she felt urged to tear her Bible up. She often found she could neither eat nor sleep and was continually haunted by the thought of committing suicide. She lived in a state of perpetual strife with her mother whose Christian faith particularly riled her, and as a result of this she decided she would never become a Christian herself. She also found she hated and detested any real Christian she came into contact with. Nevertheless she occasionally attended the prayer meetings of the local church but found that the praying merely disgusted her. As a result of the depressions she was admitted to the Christian medical centre Hohe Mark in Germany. The counselling sessions, however, made her afraid and she felt so restless during the prayer times that she tried to avoid them. In the same way she found it impossible to follow the daily devotions and could neither read her Bible there nor pray, although she sometimes wanted to. If she did try to pray she felt as if she were being choked, and if another person tried to lead her in prayer she could only repeat the words with great difficulty. She found it impossible to even mention the name of Jesus and if anyone asked her to pronounce his name, something struggled within her against doing so. At the same time she felt that the idea of having faith in the sacrificial death of Christ was merely a man-made doctrine.

The patient's condition definitely pointed to something more than a mere neurotic rejection of her mother. Besides, there were also no evident signs that she was suffering from hysteria. Her statements about her past life were always both calm and factual. In addition to this, psychotherapeutic treatment produced no improvement in her condition. Thus it became obvious that she was really suffering as a result of the demonic. She even felt herself that the was under a kind of spell, and this was further supported by her statement that at night she sometimes heard footsteps coming up to her bed and had the feeling that a figure was approaching her trying to squeeze her throat or put its hands on her chest. Since it was the steps themselves that usually woke her up, she was always wide awake during this experience. When the Christian who was counselling her saw that she genuinely wanted to repent, he commanded the devil to leave her alone. At once the woman discovered she could pray and speak to Christ, and she experienced a definite feeling of relief and deliverance which continued later.

The peculiar phenomena which Johann Blumhardt noticed in the case of Gottliebin Dittus led him to a similar conclusion. Yet no doubt even the majority of

Christian psychiatrists would still only regard these examples as extreme cases of hysteria or imagined possession. However, I am convinced that Gottliebin Dittus was really possessed, particularly on account of the facts that on more than one occasion strange voices were heard to speak out of her using languages she normally had no knowledge of, that they uttered blasphemous and derisive things, and since poltergeists were frequently heard in her vicinity by independent witnesses. For example several council officials from Möttlingen together with the doctor who treated her, stayed at her house one night and heard the sound of blows and knockings, and also saw a table move by itself. In spite of the thorough investigation which followed, no satisfactory explanation was ever found. But as we have already mentioned, it is just this type of ghost-like phenomenon that occurs so often in conjunction with possession. Also included among the hysterical neuroses is an imaginary form of possession which, if confused with a genuine case of possession can lead to disastrous results. An unnerving example of this took place only recently, and you can find references to it in my two books 'Die Prüfung der Geister' and 'Zum Kampf gegen die Pfingstbewegung'. In my own experience I have found that instances of pseudopossession occur much more frequently than genuine cases of possession. In fact pseudopossession played quite a considerable part at the birth of the Pentecostal movement, although real instances of possession were not unknown then. In a similar way the Catholic Church has also been guilty of often confusing hysterical possession with actual possession, probably because she attaches much more significance to the phenomenon of possession than does the Protestant Church which seems to almost ignore the subject completely.

If a very impressionable person, and particularly a woman, is in a situation where the devil or demons

and possession are being talked about a great deal, or if
an actual story of possession is circulating in the neighbourhood, then the person can easily be overcome by
the fear that he too may fall into the devil's hands, and
he may even begin to imagine that he is himself possessed. On the other hand a person may become the
victim of an unconscious desire to be possessed in order
to draw attention to himself and obtain the sympathy
of his fellows. This may even involve him in subscribing
himself to the devil as a kind of game, whereby using
his imagination and acting ability he will quite often
successfully try to convince those around him that he
is actually possessed. He may writhe on the floor, rage
and scream, begin to curse and blaspheme, and even
start pouring scorn on the Christian faith and generally act as if the very devil himself were living within him.
If an attempt is made at exorcism, and he is asked why
the demons have entered him, or what their names are,
and how many there are, or when they will leave, and
so on, he will give answers corresponding to what he
imagines real demons would say in the circumstances.
Usually it soon becomes quite obvious what his intentions
are. For example he may tell the exorcist to stop attempting to drive the demons out, or he may on the other
hand predict the exact date the spirits will depart, or
allow the 'demon' to speak about his fear of judgement
and damnation — yet all the time he speaks, his tone of
voice will remain exactly the same as that which is
characteristic of him in normal life. After a sustained
time of prayer the patient may suddenly begin to cough
in a peculiar way which is meant to indicate that the
'demon' is now being driven out. This type of behaviour
can be very contagious amongst a group of suggestible
people. Not surprisingly then, it is not unusual to find
that one such sufferer can often spark off a whole
epidemic of pseudo-possession.

By acting in the way we have just described, however, the person who is only suffering from an imaginary form of possession reveals certain characteristics which distinguish his illness quite clearly from a real case of possession. For the first thing the statements made by a hysterically 'possessed' person are of a thoroughly human nature. It can be demonstrated that the words uttered by the 'demons' in the 'possessed' person are either the product of his own imagination or else the result of certain impressions made on his subconscious mind by the outside world. Similarly, if the patient in his detailed monologue or in his animated conversation with the counsellor fails to speak in a foreign language in which he is not fluent, the likelihood of pseudopossession is greatly increased. Finally, if the person appears to be quite a normal and happy individual when he is not actually in the presence of the counsellor, this is also indicative of an imaginary case of possession.

Ex. 12. An extremely impressionable and suggestible patient used to fall into a trance during church services or when people prayed. She would then in a rather theatrical way begin to utter the messages of a demon that was supposedly living within her. However, her trances in fact proved to be a form of self-hypnosis and the voice that spoke out of her was evidently no different from her normal speaking voice, neither in tone nor diction. In the same way, the content of what she said corresponded exactly to an experience buried in her subconscious mind which was later brought to the surface through exhaustive inquiries being made into her mental and emotional life. Her trances were therefore not demonic disturbances of her consciousness, but rather a subconscious counterfeit. When the patient was made to realize the true background of her complaint, the trance-like states and the utterances of the 'demon' soon disappeared.

V. Psychopathy or the Demonic?

We must now consider what our attitude should be towards the abnormal characteristics of those people whose emotions fail to fit them for society as we know it. This would include the excitation and aggressiveness of the inadequate, the spite and schemes of the hysterical person, the lack of honesty of the compulsive liar, the sexual aberration of the pervert, and the violence of the drug addict. The question which faces us is, are these symptoms basically of a psychopathic nature with only a similarity to the demonic, or are they really symptoms of demonic subjection occurring in a psychopathic guise?

First of all on medical grounds one can assume that symptoms of the nature we have just described are probably indicative of an endogenous pathological emotional disturbance. Yet it is just this type of emotionally unstable person that the devil attempts to lead into sin and bind to himself. He uses the person's abnormal disposition as a welcome point of attack. As a result of this, the psychopath who constantly commits these forms of amoral conduct can easily fall victim to a demonic form of bondage. For this reason one frequently finds psychopathy and demonic subjection occurring simultaneously, so much so that the two conditons are often almost indistinguishable. Thus when we find psychopathic symptoms present in a person we should not merely be content to assume that he is suffering from some emotional or pathological trouble, but we should ask ourselves to what extent the demonic is involved possibly in the form of an occult oppression.

The difficulty experienced in answering the question, psychopathy or the demonic, is illustrated in the following example.

Ex. 13. A disabled ex-service man in his fifties was excitable and easily depressed. His grandfather had

suffered from depressions and had finally committed
suicide. His father had been similarly afflicted, had had
a quick temper, and as a child had been charmed against
an illness. The patient himself suffered his first depression
when he was 22 years old. As a result of this he had gone
to a fortune-teller whose predictions were actually
fulfilled. In the second world war after going through
a very trying experience, he suffered a second depression.
As soon as he senses he is being misunderstood by others
he becomes noisy and excited, and starts making spiteful
comments about them, so much so that they tend to draw
back from him. However, this makes him even more
sensitive and he begins to blame other people entirely
for his state of anxiety, refusing any attempt at reconciliation. In comparison to this when the patient is
free from agitation he is quiet and sociable, recognizes
his own faults, is concerned about the feelings of others,
and is always willing to apologize when he has acted
wrongly. At the same time he will be kind and helpful
to people and will often be prepared to give his testimony
as a Christian. Sooner or later, however, he gets angry
and excited over some triviality and once more begins
to despair of life. If the source of his agitation is removed
or if someone encourages him in love, he quietens down
again quickly.

Here we have an example in which it is very difficult
to tell whether the complaint is that of an endogenous
and inherited pathological illness or the result of some
contact the family has had with occultism which is
causing or at least triggering off his reactions.

There are, however, certain symptoms which we can
mention that will help us to distinguish between cases of
psychopathy and the demonic.

If a person expresses continual regret for his agitation,
or dishonesty, or moodiness, one can immediately discard
all thought of the demonic. In the same way none of

the phobias or habits of the obsessional patient, nor the shyness and inhibitions of the insecure, nor the unrestrained actions of the hypomanic psychopath, nor the fearful introspection of the hypochondriac, can be attributed to the work of the demonic. On the other hand any violent action which the patient suddenly performs under oaths and curses, any strong addiction from which the patient neither can nor wants to free himself, is often a sign that the devil has taken hold of him in some way.

If, however, authoritative counselling produces little or no real improvement in his condition, then one must reckon again with some endogenous psychopathic illness. When the illness is sufficiently advanced, the symptoms will continue to recur no matter how much the patient would like to be liberated from them. On the other hand, if the demonic is the root cause of the problem, then the symptoms will immediately begin to disappear after the patient has mustered up enough strength to make an open confession of his sins, to pray a prayer of renunciation, and to cut himself off from the source of his bondage.

VI. *Senile Dementia or the Demonic?*

The question of the demonic often arises in the case of elderly people. Since arteriosclerosis of the brain vessels usually results in an impediment in the person's ability to concentrate, his prayer life and Bible reading will correspondingly suffer. Elderly people therefore frequently lack the joy that was once theirs when they prayed. It becomes an effort to pray now and the person quite often finds the effort too much for him in spite of the fact that he realizes how important the matter of prayer is in maintaining one's relationship with God. Feeling his Christian life has lost a lot of its vitality, he will begin to reproach himself, and yet his condition will have nothing to do with the demonic, but will only be the result of some pathological changes which have taken place in his body.

One must be very clear in one's mind concerning the difference between this type of pathological illness and a genuine attack of the devil which a believer might experience, particularly when he is very ill or on his death bed. The devil knows full well that when a man reaches old age he is often more easily susceptible to certain temptations. Thus in order to destroy his relationship with God, the devil will try to instil into him a strong aversion to prayer and doubts concerning the Word of God and his own faith. If this is the case, the person may find that as he is reading his Bible the thought suddenly enters his mind that it is all nonsense. On the other hand the devil may try to persuade the person that he is lost and that God has forsaken him, or he may attack him with sexual thoughts and temptations which the person may find very difficult to overcome. This can lead to depression. Similarly some unpleasant memory may begin to torment him and make him feel that God has withdrawn Himself from him. He may feel that Satan is using all these temptations to lead him into despair and even suicide. However, this state of mind has nothing to do with demonic subjection or possession, for as we mentioned at the very outset, these two conditions only develop in the lives of people who have consciously or unconsciously turned their backs on God. Hence the believer who reaches old age and finds himself subject to temptations of this nature must not allow himself to be led into a state of depression. If he will but continually call upon God when the temations arise, or even command the enemy himself in the name of Jesus to depart, the devil will flee from him and the temptations usually recede quite quickly.

VII. *Caution in Questionable Cases of the Demonic*

We have tried to show in the arguments presented, and
in particular through what we have mentioned about
imaginary possession, how easy it is to arrive at a false
diagnosis if one fails to exercise sufficient care when
seeking to assess the demonic. One must be especially
careful in this area, for the distinguishing between disease
and the demonic is not only a very difficult task but also
a very responsible one. While on the one hand one must
be completely impartial when approaching the question
of the demonic, it is imperative on the other hand not
to diagnose demonic subjection and even more so
possession, without making a thorough-going investigation
of the causes beforehand. Unfortunately there are many
Christians who are all too ready to accept the presence
of the demonic in doubtful cases of emotional disturbance.
Their diagnosis is open to doubt from the very outset
if one finds that none of the underlying causes we have
already mentioned are present. And even if it can be
clearly demonstrated that the parents for example have
taken part in occult practices, or that the patient himself
has committed grave sins, this is still not definite proof
that the demonic is involved, and further investigation is
still necessary. The really crucial thing for this type of
diagnosis is to prove after one has excluded the possibility
of pathological disturbance, the presence of several of the
underlying causes we have outlined in the first section
of this part of the book.

Another reason for taking particular care in diagnosing
the demonic is the fact that frequently the people one
is dealing with are by nature very sensitive and emotional.
If such a person is told glibly that Satan has bound him or
even possessed him, this reproach can itself lead to much
restlessness, fear, and depression in the patient. In particular, if a Christian whose spiritual life has been para-

lysed by the pathological restraints of his melancholic illness, or whose mind is plagued with blasphemous thoughts, is told by a counsellor that he is under a ban of the devil, one can understand why the person will believe even more strongly that he is eternally lost, the more so if an attempt to 'drive the demons out' fails. I have witnessed on numerous occasions the adverse effects produced on emotionally ill people when they have been incorrectly diagnosed as suffering from demonic subjection. To further burden a person suffering from a mental illness by telling him that he has fallen into the hands of the devil is inexcusable. Anyone who voices an opinion of this nature without having any knowledge of abnormal mental behaviour is not only acting very rashly but may also be subjecting the patient to an untold amount of cruelty. I heard once from a person who had been staying at a Christian convalescent home, that a patient had been admitted while she was there who had exhibited the well-known signs of mental depression and melancholia. However, after the man in charge of the home had had a short talk with the new arrival, he diagnosed his complaint as demonic subjection, and when subsequent counselling had no effect on the patient's condition, he was sent back home after only a few days. I have witnessed stories similar to this personally.

While it is true that one must initially show great restraint when investigating a case of suspected demonic subjection, if it becomes transparently clear that the demonic is present, then the person concerned must be told quite definitely, but in love, that Satan has bound him to himself. Even if the patient is unwilling to accept this or shows signs of alarm, one must still not withhold the truth from him, and any resulting shock will only have a wholesome effect in the end. The patient must be made to realize who the enemy of his soul really is,

and then together with the counsellor and if possible
a group of praying Christians he must set out to resist
this enemy.

Since the distinguishing between pathological and demonic disturbances involves grave responsibilities one
is urgently advised in all doubtful cases to call in the help
of a qualified Christian psychiatrist or counsellor who
has had experience in these matters. One should moreover
pray for the gift of discernment which is one of the gifts
of the Spirit mentioned in 1 Corinthians 12. In the last
analysis it is only the Spirit of God who can impart to
us a real understanding of the plight of those who turn
to us for help, and it is only He who can prevent us from
saying things and acting in a way that may not only be
incorrect but also harmful.

D. CHRISTIAN FAITH AND THE DEMONIC

Finally we must consider three questions that are frequently being asked by Christian people.

I. *Can a Christian Suffer from Demonic Subjection?*

Although the opinion is often expressed that the devil
can bind Christians as well as non-Christians to himself, one must point out that the Bible itself fails to
record one single case where a follower of Christ has
become oppressed by the devil while living a life in
obedience to his Master. In fact in the case of Mary
Magdalene, although she was possessed by seven demons
(Mk. 16:9; Luke 8:2), when she came into contact with
Jesus she was delivered from her bondage. So one finds
that just as the houses which had their door-posts and
lintels sprinkled with blood at the time of the Exodus had

nothing to fear from the angel of destruction (Ex. 12:13), so too every believer who lays claim to the blood of Christ as a covering for his own sin, is protected from the subjection of the devil. If a person abides under the blood of Christ, the enemy has no possibility of reaching him. Every believer who walks in the inexhaustible forgiving grace of the Lord Jesus has been delivered and will be delivered from every dominion of darkness (Col. 1:13–14).

Yet the stories of Ananias and Saphira, and of Judas Iscariot, make it quite clear that even real Christians or people who have been chosen by Christ for a particular ministry, if they consciously resist the Spirit of God and fall into sin without seeking forgiveness, the result can be that they succumb more and more to the devil's influence till in the end he has bound them to himself or even possessed them. In the case of Ananias and Saphira, through seeking to lie to the Holy Spirit they presented the devil with his opportunity (Acts 5:3, 4), while in Judas' case it was his continued love of money and theft that instigated his downfall (John 12:6, Luke 12:3). It is possible for people in these circumstances to repent as Judas did when he recognized and confessed his sin and tried to make restitution, but in his case the devil was able to convince him that his guilt was too great and that he could no longer hope to be forgiven. Nothing else remained for him than to take his own life. Thus failing to turn to God and ask for forgiveness, he proceeded to execute divine judgement upon himself.

II. *Can a Demonically Oppressed Person be Delivered, and if so, How?*

In Christian circles one can often hear it said that since Satan exercises so much power over people today, many

are unreceptive to the gospel since the devil has blinded
their eyes or produced an animosity in their hearts towards God. Therefore it is said that it is almost pointless
to pray for such people since they are surrounded by
such a host of demonic forces that the Christian's prayers
will almost certainly fail to reach the ears of God.
However, such an outlook is merely a sign of a pronounced
lack of faith. Every Christian who seeks to oppose the
enemy by relying on the victory that Christ achieved and
who persists in his struggle to free the demonically
oppressed, can be certain his prayers will be answered.
And any person who accepts Jesus as his Lord and
Saviour, and who makes it his aim to follow Him, will
be able to find deliverance from all forms of demonic
oppression. In cases where the oppression is still in its
early stages, deliverance usually occurs either during the
first or the first few counselling sessions. If, however, the
person concerned has committed certain grave sins, or
if the counsellor fails to make use of all the armour of
God and lacks a vital knowledge of real Christian warfare,
then deliverance may only be finally achieved after a
considerable interval of time. Similarly if the oppressed
person is unprepared to surrender himself completely to
Christ, he leaves Satan certain footholds in his life,
which possibly in conjunction with some endogenous
weakness in his emotions or personality may initially
result in his deliverance being incomplete. A person in
this situation can easily give one the impression of being
born again through certain changes which start taking
place in his character, but he will be unconscious of the
subtle attacks and promptings of the devil which will
make him from time to time do things against his own
will. It is true, he no longer loves sin, and yet he will
still find himself doing the evil that he hates (Rom.
7:15, 19). If this is the case, then a remnant of the
demonic remains. This means that although the person

is not in bondage to the devil any longer, the devil nevertheless still attempts to seduce him in all sorts of ways in order to captivate him again. And he is sometimes successful. The seduction becomes apparent in that the subjected person's besetting sins recur from time to time. Thus for example, he may be gripped afresh perhaps by spitefulness or dishonesty, bitterness, complaint against God, a longing for physical pleasure, or hypersensitivity and panic, and mediumistic abilities may also persist for some time as well. Then on top of this, even if the person does not usually suffer from depressions, the thought and even the desire to commit suicide may frequently fill his mind.

It is surprising how often one can meet people in whom this type of demonic remnant is still to be found. We will quote just one example.

Ex. 14. Ever since her youth a patient had been committing grave sexual perversions. For years she had suffered from a clear form of demonic bondage, mainly as a result of the influence of her demonically subjected father. In her own strength she found it impossible to free herself from her troubles, until one day she came into contact with a Christian. She subsequently turned to Christ and was freed from her sin. After a while, however, she was brought into bondage to the devil again, and began to turn back to the sin which still held a peculiar attraction for her. This continued for some years. In the end through the correspondence of a certain minister and through regularly listening to a gospel broadcast, she was again greatly helped and experienced a definite improvement in her condition, which has lasted now for a number of years. And yet the devil still refuses to leave her in peace. Each evening before she goes to sleep he thrusts sexual pictures into her mind and simultaneously for no reason at all instils her with fear, persuading her to contemplate suicide. In order to resist the devil's attacks, the woman tells him she wants nothing more to do with his ideas and she resorts to prayer. The sin which has been a snare to her for years, she now abhors, but in spite of this she still occasionally falls victim to it. In a similar way her suicidal thoughts keep recurring together with her unfounded fears. She is convinced that the devil is responsible for her thoughts and relapses, and that he is by means of them seeking to get her into his power again.

However, the more the Spirit of God takes control of the life of a believer, the more victories that believer will be able to experience. And yet if the devil sees that he is about to lose one of his captives, he may launch a number of last minute offences in order if possible to prevent his victim slipping from his grasp when he makes his decisive step of faith. This may result in the patient experiencing a considerable emotional crisis, so much so that he may be in danger of a serious relapse. Yet with the counsellor's help if the person makes a complete and final committal of his life into the Saviour's hands, and if the enemy is commanded to leave in the name of Jesus, the final victory is always Christ's.

The believer will nevertheless continue to be tempted by the enemy of the souls of men. However, he will now no longer be forced to commit sin as was the case when he was in bondage to the devil, but will retain his freedom to act as he chooses. Instead of removing a person from temptation, the Holy Spirit rather gives the follower of Christ the ability to resist the devil and to abhor sin, so much so that Satan is forced to flee (James 4:7). The 'fiery darts of the wicked one' bounce off the shield of faith of the born again Christian. He is freed from the law of sin, for his sinful passions are mortified by the Spirit of God (Rom. 8:2—13). From now on if he succumbs to temptation it is because he has been caught unawares, for at heart he no longer wishes to sin. Yet if he does sin, he can immediately repent and is assured of God's forgiveness through which all unforgiven sin in his life can be covered. In this way Satan's right of entry into his life is removed once and for all.

Since the words 'bondage', 'seduction' and 'temptation' are frequently misapplied, it is essential that we should be aware of the differences between these three terms. Whereas in the case of 'bondage', and to a lesser extent in the case of 'seduction' one is entitled to think of a demonic background to the trouble, in the case of 'temptation' this is never possible (James 1:14, 15; 2 Tim. 2:26; John 13:2, 27).

III. *Can Contact with the Demonically Oppressed and Intercession for Them be Dangerous in any Spiritual, Mental or even Physical Way?*

This question relating to the dangers involved in counselling and contacting the demonically oppressed is quite often raised by Christians, and goes back basically to the problem of the transference of evil forces. To prove their point of view, people often refer to the fact that many of those who intercede for the demonically oppressed ultimately fall prey to depressions, anxiety states and similar trials themselves. However, there is no record at all in the Bible of the transference of evil forces on to believers. In the story of the seven sons of Sceva in Acts 19 which is often brought forward as evidence for this idea, although the evil spirit leaped on them and injured them, one must realize that these men were not in fact followers of Christ but rather itinerant Jewish exorcists who were only using the name of Jesus to drive out demons in order to enhance their own name. In this example the words of Jesus in Matthew 7:28, 29 are particularly applicable. Concerning injury being done to genuine followers of Christ the Scriptures are likewise as silent. On the contrary one finds that Jesus expressly promised his own that no one would be able to snatch them out of either his Father's or His own hands (John 10:28, 29). In addition to this He states that he has given them authority over all the power of the enemy and that nothing will be able to harm them (Luk. 10:19). Paul, writing in a similar vein, says that the Lord is faithful and will strengthen and guard the Christian from the evil one (2 Thess. 3:3), and that neither principalities nor powers will separate him from the love of God in Christ Jesus (Rom. 8:38).

Similarly the often repeated warning that intercession for the demonically oppressed is dangerous finds no support in the pages of the Bible. On the contrary the Scriptures exhort us to offer up supplications, prayers, intercessions, and thanksgivings for all men (1. Tim. 2:1). There seems to be only one exception to this, and that is in the case where a person has committed a 'sin unto death', whereby he consciously and unrepentantly rejects the Lord Jesus. For such a person John does not say we ought to pray (1 John 5:16), but only because in these circumstances there remains no forgiveness for sins (Heb. 10:26—30) and not because intercession in this case would result in some form of injury to the one who intercedes.

For these reasons the Christian who comes into contact with people who are demonically oppressed, or who prays for such people, need have no fear of being harmed so long as he is living in vital contact with his Lord, and by faith claims the promises of the Scriptures we have just outlined.

However, it is true to say that a demon may temporarily be able to frighten an emotionally unstable Christian who is resisting his influence through prayer, by submitting him to certain ghostlike experiences, or by attacking his Christian life in a host of different ways, or by sowing discord between him and his friends. Anyone therefore joining in a battle for the deliverance of an oppressed person must reckon on the devil attempting to take his revenge. However, by learning to recognize his satanic influences immediately they appear, one will with God's help be able to fend off all his fiery darts. To allow oneself to be intimidated by these devilish attacks would be a sign of a lack of faith. A Christian should never be afraid of interceding for a person in bondage, for if he were, it would only prove he thought more of his own welfare than for that of the subjected person. Our duty is to take hold of the shield of faith, to put on the helmet of salvation and to join battle with the enemy, and to fight the fight of faith.

Yet we have still to explain why a number of people who have interceded for the demonically subjected or who have had close contact with them, have apparently been affected by this contact and why they have sometimes suffered from severe anxiety states and similar such trials for a considerable time afterwards. In my own experience the people who have suffered in this way have usually been of an impressionable nature and of an anxious disposition. If a person like this hears talk of the transference of demonic powers, or is warned against praying for subjected people, and is then confronted by someone he believes to be demonically oppressed, he can easily succumb to an acute state of fear and restlessness, and start noticing all sorts of physical and nervous complaints in himself, which he will regard as having a demonic origin. However, the complaints will often only be the product of the person's own fear of a possible demonic transference. This becomes obvious when the person is counselled and the cause of his anxieties explained to him, for his complaints

thereupon soon disappear. They only persist if he ad-
heres to his conviction that they are of a demonic nature.
In the case of a Christian who is both mentally and
emotionally well-balanced, contact with demonically
oppressed people produces no ill-effects either physically
or emotionally.

As an example of this we find that Johann Blumhardt
at the end of his spiritual battle for the soul of Gottliebin Dittus was able to write to his superiors, "The
greater the strain, the greater I sensed the protection of
God around me, so much so that even after 40 hours
of struggling in prayer and fasting I felt not the slightest
tiredness nor exhaustion." Together with others with
whom I have prayed I have experienced this same
protection of the Lord when engaged in the battle for
those who are in bondage to the devil. Experience proves
that true disciples of Christ are guarded from the attacks
of the evil one (1 John 5:18, 19), and we know that Jesus
himself who is our Great High Priest prays to his father
that we will be kept from the evil one (John 17:15). Paul
too, right up to the time of his death was filled with
the assured faith that the Lord would continue to rescue
him from every evil and save him for his heavenly kingdom (2 Tim. 4:18).

And so the Christian who trusts in the overshadowing
power of his Lord need have no fear of praying for and
talking to those who are demonically oppressed. Satan
can do nothing to the Christian who remains faithful in
prayer to his Master, yet even if the prince of this world
were able to do his very worst, the Lord's disciples would
still be able to sing in joyful confidence with Martin
Luther:

And though the world with devils filled
Should threaten to undo us,
We will not fear for God has willed
His truth to triumph through us. Hallelujah!